The Gain: Finding Gratitude in the Pain

Copyright © 2025 Remy Scott Marks

All rights reserved. No part of this book may be reproduced or used in any manner without written permission of the copyright owner, except for the use of brief quotations in a book review.

To request permission or for more information, contact:

Remy Scott Marks
remyscottmarks@gmail.com

ISBN: 9798309033362

First Edition February 2025

Table of Contents

Section One: Grief

Grief: Who is She? 7
(P.A.I.N.) 9
Decomposition 11
Seroquel 13
Half Dead 15
Shape Shifter 17
Overdose 19
Acid Grieflux 21
Ocean 23
Lemon Tree 25
Macaroni Penguin 27

Section Two: Anger

Anger: Who is She? 29
Angel of Death 30
Angel of Hope 31
House of Lies 33
Imposter 35
Hypocrite 37
The Bigger Person 39
Human Monster 41
Return to Sender 43
Human Diary 45
Empty Parking Lot 47
Solitary Confinement 49

Section Three: Initiation

Initiation: Who is He? 51
Healing 53
Becoming 55
Claws 57
Giraffe 59
Breadcrumbs 61
Home 63
She is 65
Buried Alive 67
Shedding 69
The Gain 71

Section Four: Nirvana

Nirvana: Who is He? 73
The Deep Knows 75
200 Ladies 77
Arrival 79
No Hands 81
The Remedy 83
River 85
Giver. Of. Direction 87
Liberation 89
Rebirth 91
Sister 93
Water 95

Answer Key 97

*For my sister, Annabel,
my dear friend, Christina,
and anyone that has ever felt like they
couldn't survive the pain.*

Preface

All of the poems in this book are my own feelings and experiences with grief, anger, heartbreak, spirituality, love, peace, and faith. As the title explains, this book is about finding gratitude in the midst of the most agonizing pain. The year this book was written, I experienced many forms of loss and setbacks, the main one being a break up with my first love. The grief that I felt was so potent, all I could do was write. I am not a professional writer, nor do I have a degree in English from some prominent University. I have my Master's in Social Work, experienced immense pain and grief, and needed an outlet. The book is divided into four sections: Grief, Anger, Initiation, and Nirvana. These sections are an acronym that spell out GAIN, the title of the book, but the sections are also my personal experience finding myself and my perception of God. Additionally, each section of the book starts with a "Who is?" poem that describes a character trait as a person. These character traits are, in my opinion, the hidden character traits behind my experience in each section. The point of these "Who is?" poems is for the reader to guess which character trait I am describing and check their answers in the back of the book. I have no monopoly on healing – I am and will always be in the process of my own healing. My only hope is that this book finds at least one person who reads my words and feels less alone.

SECTiON 1: GRiEF

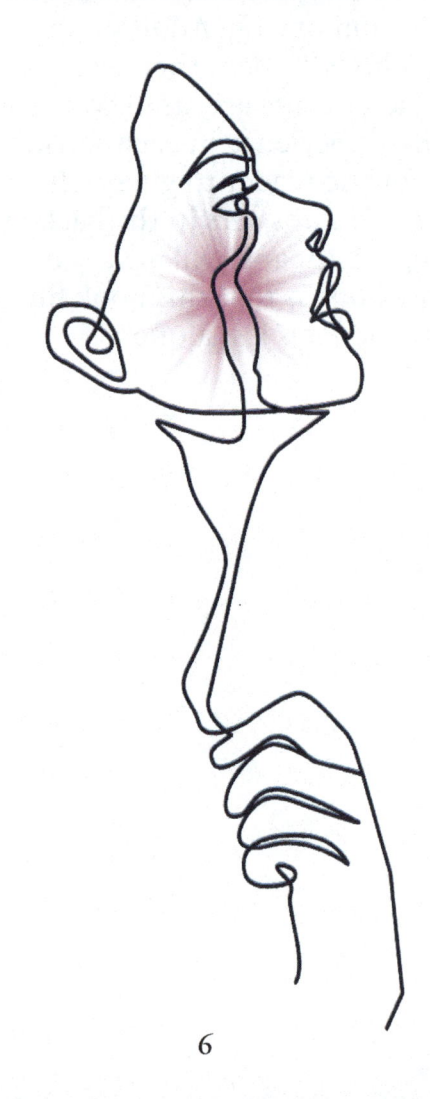

Grief: Who is She?

Despite the small age gap
She's the older cousin you admire
That is effortlessly herself
An authenticity destined to inspire

The summer's spent at Grandma's
That you'd sneak a cookie before dinner
She'd just place her hand on your shoulder
And you'd feel like the world's worst sinner

She has an extremely calming presence
Like she walks among the clouds
With nothing heavy to weigh Her down
Her freedom rarely has her on the ground

Growing up, she never played games
Not a fan of tricking or pretending
Always wore her heart on her sleeve
What she said, was what she was intending

Even when it's quite difficult
She always expresses her real feelings
Not afraid of being vulnerable
Something about Her is very healing

She never has an ulterior motive
What you see is what you get
Although, I rarely gamble
I am confident she is the safest bet

There's nothing hidden in Her brain
She always speaks up if she disagrees
With no secrets, she sleeps like a baby
We all know her, so who is She?

People. Avoiding. Internal. Nourishment. (P.A.I.N.)

The difference between misery and suffering
The former is inevitable, the latter is a choice for me
It all comes down to emotion regulation
The topic of my never-ending conversation

"Let him go"
"Walk away"
If it's meant to be, he will stay

Feel less, think more
Do what we do
Or don't bother walking back through that door

Have you ever felt like you're missing a puzzle piece?
If only you could have it, life could finally be easy
But, I'm not like them and won't ever be
The square peg/round hole concept that ensures I'm terminally unique

How can you convince someone of something they can never understand?
It's like staring at your foot and forcing it to be your hand
Or when your sickness is labeled as selfish
But, your biggest symptom is that you start to care less

Feeling lost, hopeless, and defeated
"I'm always here," but your friendship points are depleted

Conditional love, denied hugs, and shoulder shrugs
You're out of coffee, but you still need to fill their mugs

Be strong, and have faith
It will get better if you only wait
Well time is running out, and I'm drowning
I'm sorry, I'll try harder, just please stop your frowning

You, immature girl, look at your mess
One of these days, could you be yourself less?
Selfishness is all you know
Be selfless for once, it's not the "me" show

Everything you do is for the drama
One thousand excuses, your favorite is the trauma
Can you take ownership for one time in your life?
You can't blame him anymore, you're holding the knife

Don't you see what this is doing to your father?
Why can't you be his perfect daughter?
You, young lady, are the reason your life is in upheaval
Because all roads lead to pain when you try to fill a god-sized void with people

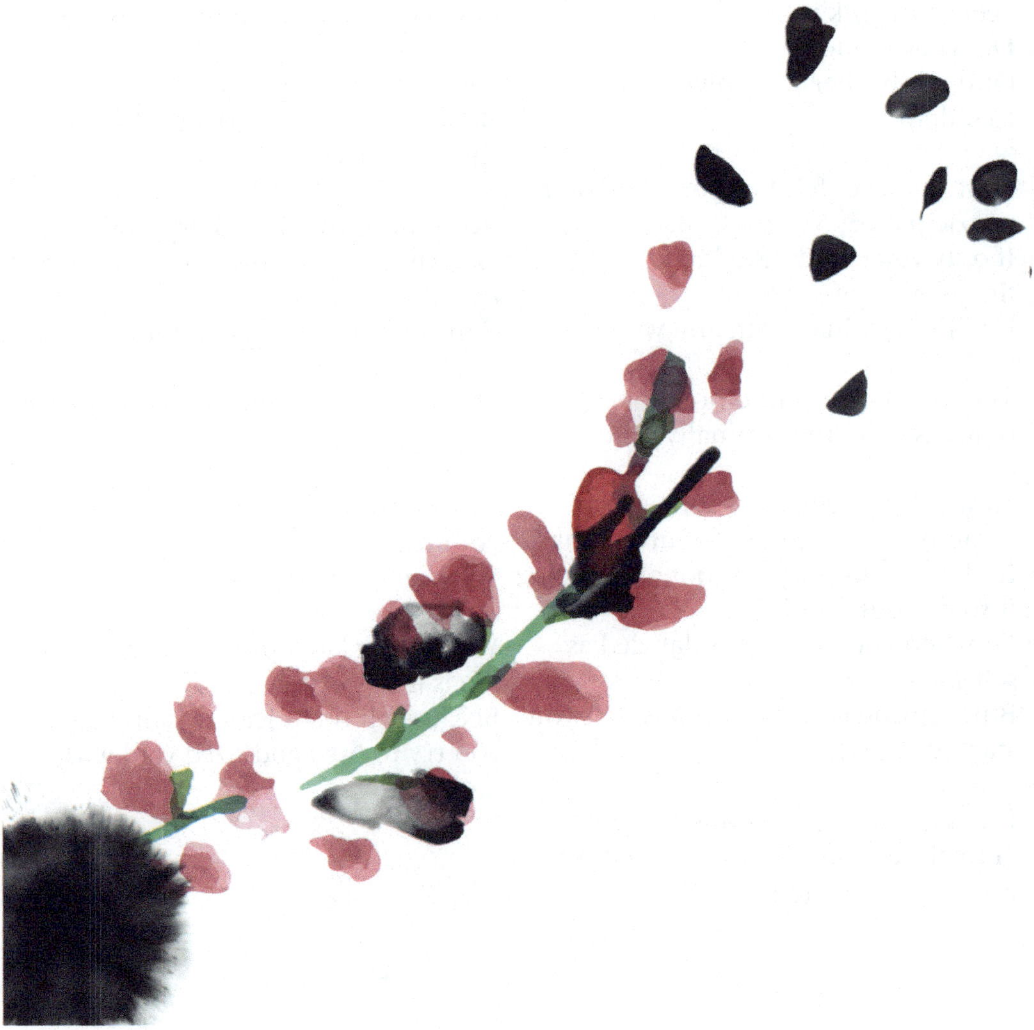

Decomposition

When your soul left your body
All the life inside me died
My love for you has rotted
Disintegrating in the tears I've cried

That fiery girl that you once knew
She's trapped inside your dark cave
Losing all she ever had
That's the risk of being brave

There is no relief from the pain
People want to call it broken
But, broken things can be fixed
In this permanent sleep, I cannot be woken

Walk away from your destruction
I cannot make you want to stay
You're enslaved to a toxic pattern
There's no reversal to the decay

You have stripped my humanity
Just a tally mark on your list
Dust where flowers once had blossomed
Best conditions for a detachment switch

Neither can live while the other survives
My innocence and what you spoiled
You gave me wings, and then you clipped them
Promising to stay, then you recoiled

Congratulations, you have won
All my nerve endings are exposed
Becoming the Voldemort you despised
All my life forces have decomposed

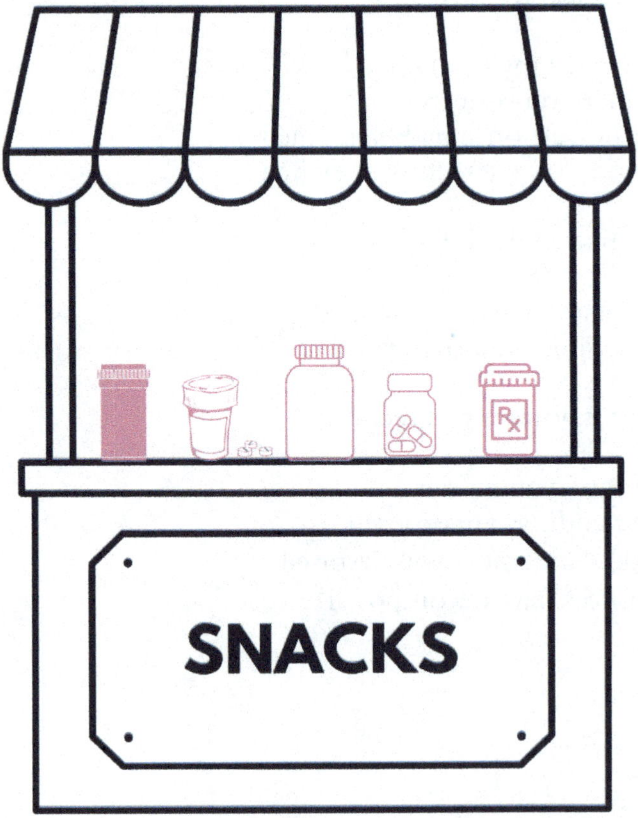
SNACKS

Seroquel

Your heart goes through the meat grinder
And no one understands
Have you prayed to God yet?
Just put this in his hands

They say suicide is selfish
To rob them of your light
But, I believe it is more inhumane
To witness my agony for another night

We put animals out of their misery
Seeing that they are hurt or wounded
Unfortunately, my debilitating heartache
Is to be tolerated, they all concluded

My family and friends believe
I will be me again one day
But, long term torture changes people
Just ask "survivors" from Guantanamo Bay

The vibrant girl they used to know
She died of smoke inhalation
Well, that's the fate of a Gaslit death
Ruled homicide, not lack of motivation

This lifeless sack of skin and bones
Will spin forever on an endless carousel
Just plastic animals and creepy music
The provided snack – Seroquel

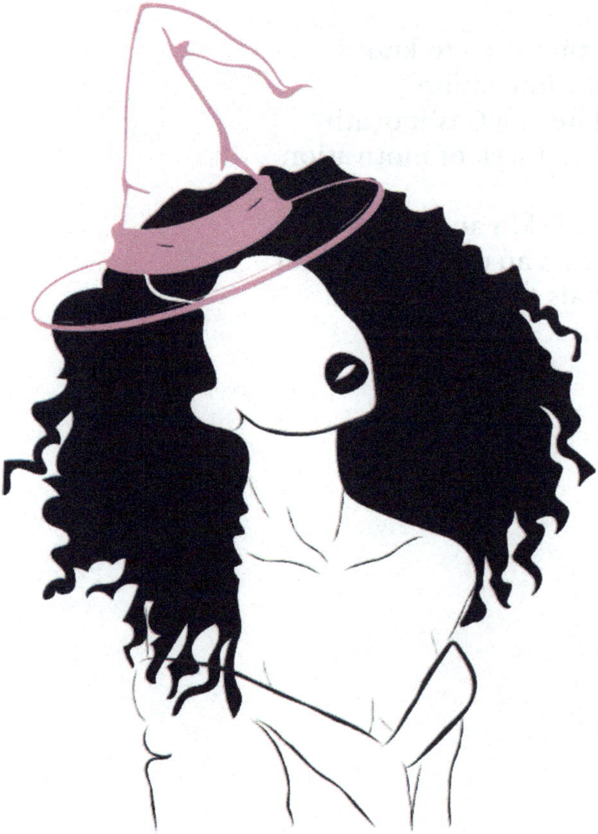

Half Dead

October is spooky season
And I feel understood
All of the ghosts and zombies
Get me like no else could

I look the same on the outside
But, my heart has turned black
After the suffering he caused me
There's no turning me back

I wander through the in-between
Where there is both life and death
My heart beating and rotting
A noticeable slowness of breath

The goblins and vampires
Nod their heads passing by
They recognize the darkness within me
A deadness in the depth of my eyes

And all the witches and monsters
No longer seem so frightening
They're honest about their motives
Around humans, I feel my chest tightening

Halloween is something twisted
You wear your mask and your disguise
The one night you pretend to be scary
But the rest of the year is your big lie

People impersonating monsters
Intentionally messing with my head
Trick or treat? Just another mind game
Either way, they leave you half dead

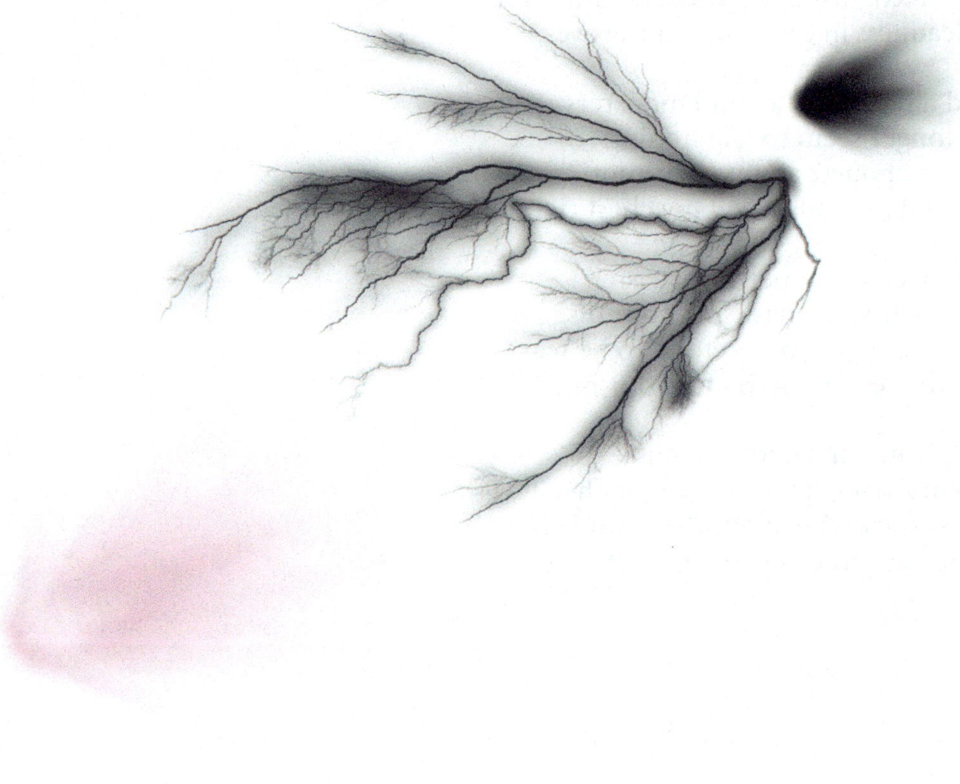

Shape Shifter

All my energy is spent
On forgetting you exist
But, before I know it
You're just a name on a list

Scorched earth in my past
Many bridges were burned
Freedom from this cycle
Is for what I have yearned

Not created nor destroyed
A transfer is what happens
As Love's evil twin
It's intensity mistook for passion

This one is different
Words I truly believe
Each time the same result
And Insanity is achieved

Always waiting in the wings
Or an ace in the hole
The enemy is one step ahead
Anyone could be the mole

At times there is hope
When I put a separation
Then comes the dilemma
Because it's death by isolation

Well, now I've learned my lesson
And this time I'll be swifter
The lies you tell yourself
When your disease is a shape shifter

Overdose

The lights that shine the brightest
Always burn out way too soon
But, even the Sun in all her power
Has to take turns with the Moon

Cunning, Baffling, and Powerful
To deceive you is the mission
It's actually quite a genius plan
Can you really be a prisoner if you don't know you're imprisoned?

Quickly learning control is an illusion
An insanity that makes you forget it even faster
When the parasite lives in your brain
One wrong move, and it becomes your master

The beast is constantly hungry
Feeding on the souls of those that suffer
Cruel, heartless, and no discrimination
Will laugh at the pleas of a crying mother

Will this hit be the last one?
A giant game of Russian Roulette
When you sell your soul to the Devil
He always comes back to collect his debts

For brief moments there is hope
When the Light casts out the darkness
But, coasting on yesterday's comfort
Is just a clever tactic to disarm us

How can the miracle be so far away?
And yet it's freedom feel so close
Always a thief in the night
The silent, soul swindle of an overdose

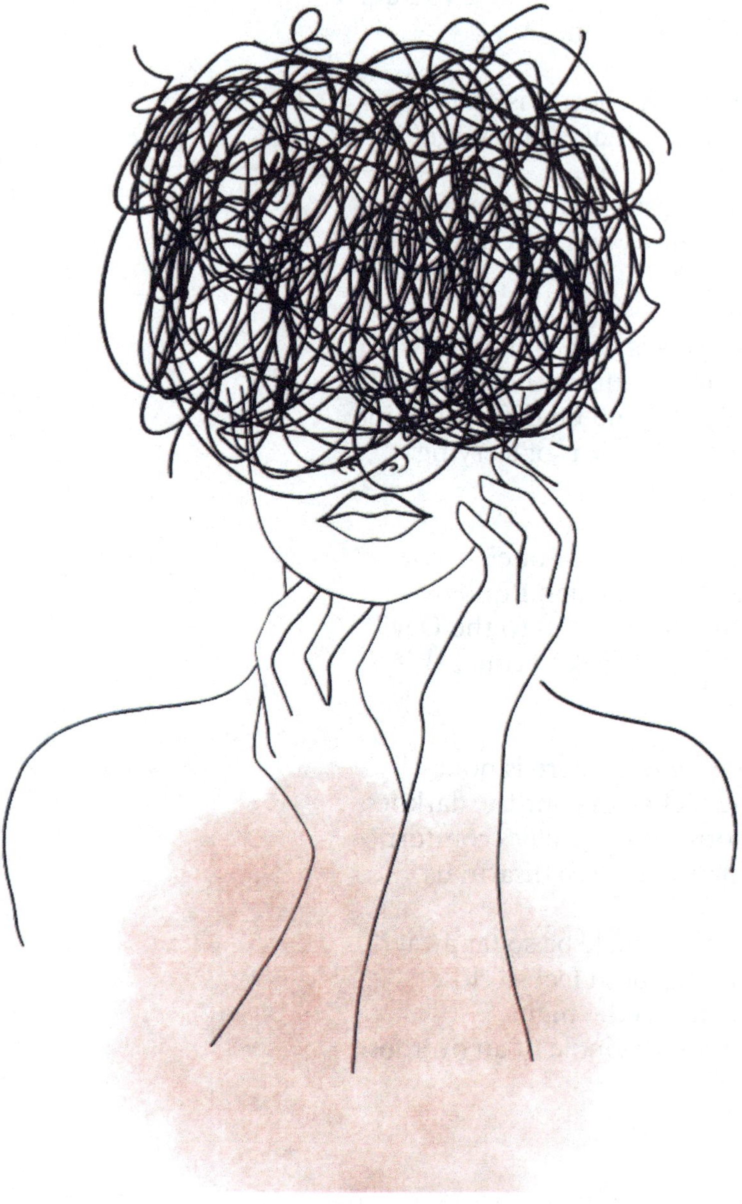

Acid Grieflux

The only certainty in this life
Is that it comes to a bitter end
No one can avoid this fate
Although, we often play pretend

Death is not the pain I fear
The Grim Reaper I would welcome
No, the suffering that I dread the most
Is the loss of others I can't escape from

My worn-out tear ducts are in a crisis
They have declared a state of drought
The loss comes faster than the healing
Time, as the solution, I'm starting to doubt

The plates of my chest start to shift
Each time I am in mourning
It causes a quake deep in my heart
The bereavement's a never-ending storming

Every crevice in my body
Is packed and stuffed up to the brim
There's nowhere else for grief to fit
It's now pulsating through every limb

With each bite of death or loss
I try to swallow and hold it down
Praying my weary body has space to hold it
But, grief is not measured by the pound

As I start to digest the last one
Another course of grief leaves me re-lief-less
Well, this time it's coming right back up
Do I take an antacid or antidepressant for my Acid Grieflux?

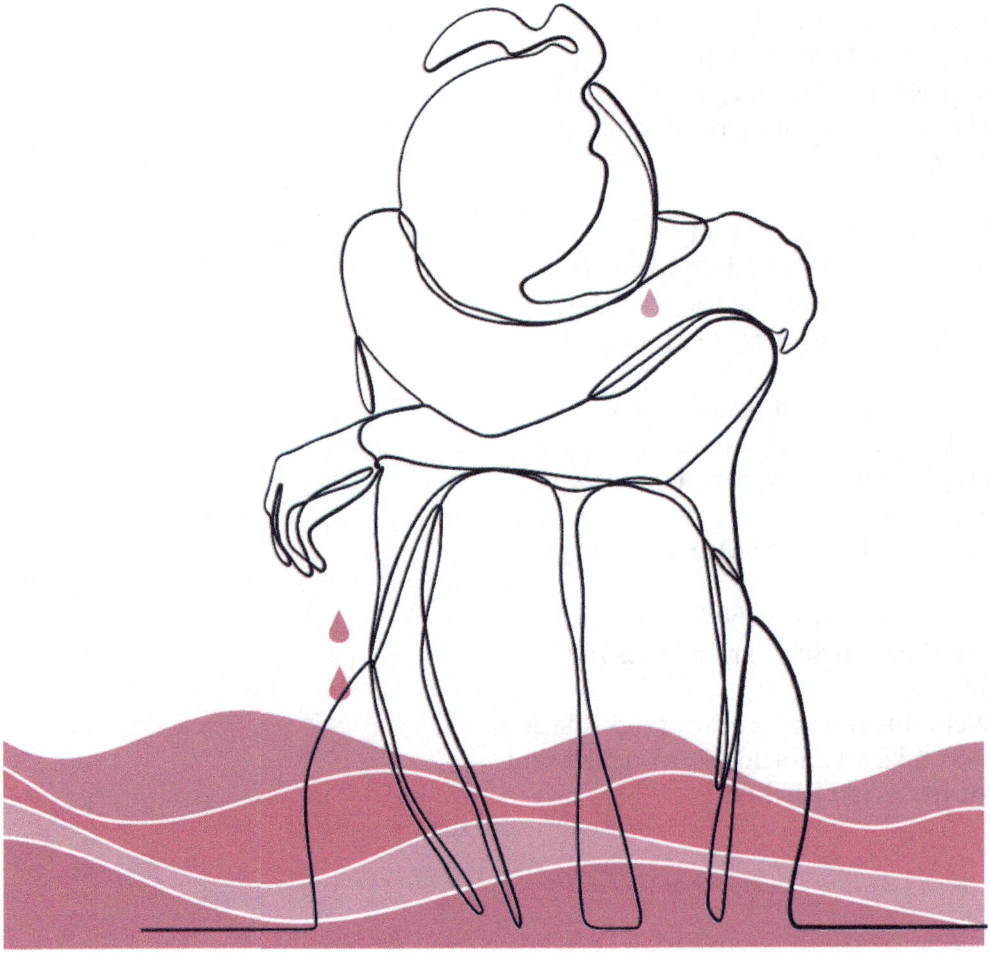

Ocean

I used to absolutely adore the ocean
Until you evoked such painful emotions
The endless nights from words unspoken
Never thought I'd miss all the commotion
Gasoline to my fire, you caused an explosion
Choose when I exist, I took the demotion
Watching all I love fade away- slow erosion
A hot Texas summer, but my heart is frozen
Bring out the ice pick & hammer till it's broken
I'm an option, but for me you're always chosen
"Get on with your life," but my life was stolen
How can I forget with the memories still woven
Each time I try harder, you punish my devotion
My resilience is still no match for the corrosion
The tears I've cried could fill an entire ocean

My eyes are swollen
I need ibuprofen
I'm extremely deficient in oxytocin
Just another tattoo of a semicolon

I used to absolutely adore the ocean.

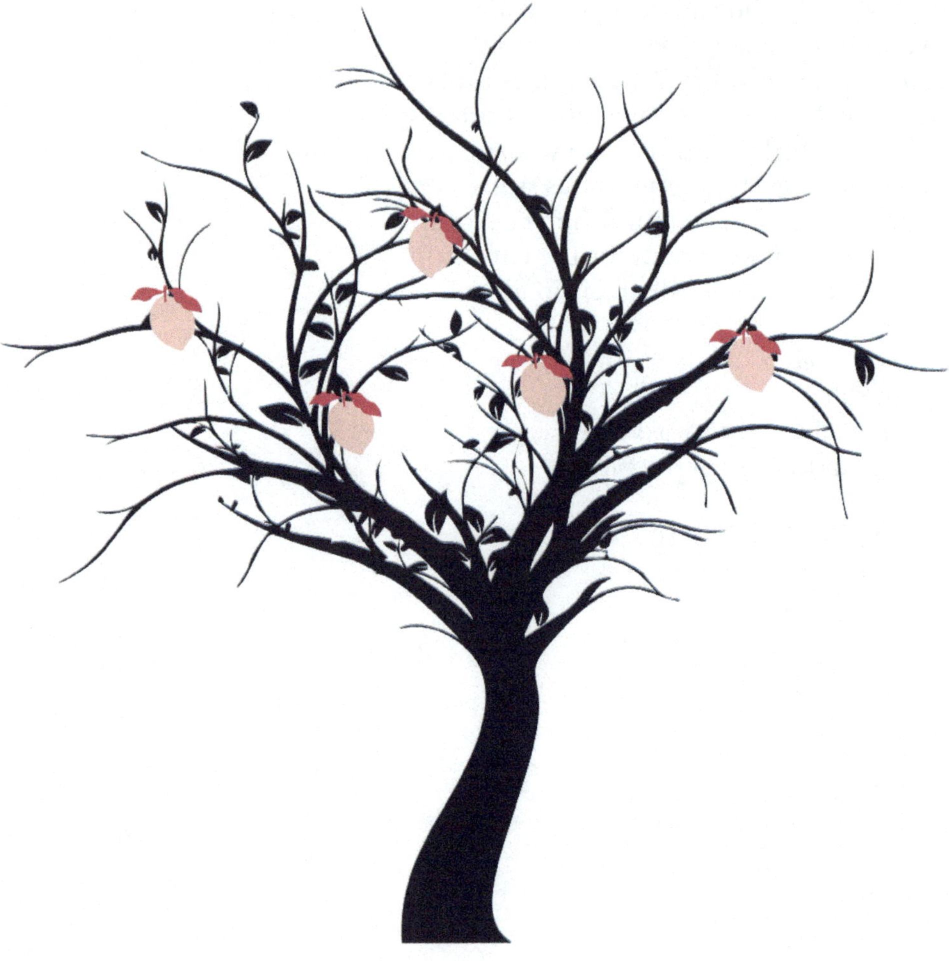

Lemon Tree

Seven years ago, we took a picture in front of a lemon tree
I wish I could have seen then, what today my world would be

Both you and the tree were vibrant with color
As if you knew a secret you only shared with the other

The pair of you were strong and bold in your roots
But, generous and compassionate in the giving of your fruits

And in the unbearable heat the Texas sun made
You still welcomed others and graciously offered your shade

That photo in my phone was taken two years to the day
That the Grim Reaper would collect & your life was to pay

It's unfathomable to understand the me in that picture
Exactly two years later, would no longer have that sister

And the lemon tree's broken heart she could not hide
For exactly three years later, she froze in an ice storm and died

Every morning, drinking my coffee, I stare at her lifeless stump
With nowhere to go, my love for you forms in my throat as a lump

I know your world was filled with pain, and I hope now you are free
I picture you laughing in the sun, laying under our lemon tree

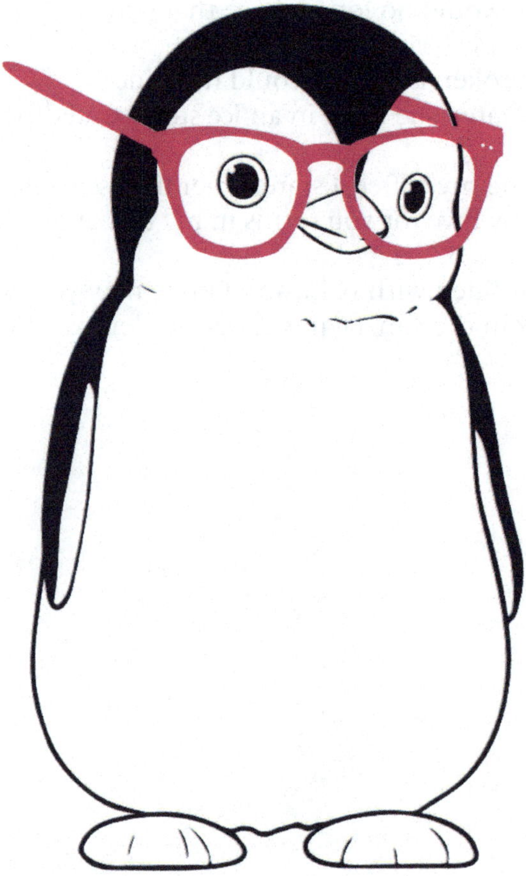

Macaroni Penguin

I was born a bird, and I will never fly
I have wings, but they cannot take me high

I once was content with just swimming
I now know I'm a bird, and contentment is dimming

All the others like me only see what has been
But, I know I'm a bird & there's a yearning to fly deep within

What is known cannot be unknown, or so they say
So, my bliss is the price for knowledge I had to pay

It's like living my entire life without being able to see
Being handed the perfect glasses, but they're taken from me

How can I feel satisfied with my blurry vision?
When I know there are glasses that let me see with precision?

I look up at the sky and see other birds flying
There's an ache in my heart that feels like I'm dying

I, too, am a bird like those soaring in the clouds
But, unlike them, the gift of flying I was not endowed

I can only waddle & swim, even if my wings I strengthen
I am a bird, but I will only ever be a macaroni penguin

SECTiON 2: ANGER

Anger: Who is She?

No matter how great Her distance
She's the old friend you have not seen
That always comes back to "comfort" you
Like it was all a part of Her master scheme

She never comes empty handed
Instead of gifts She brings you questions
The kind that erodes your very essence
Her wrapping paper made of suggestions

Never known to raise Her voice
She speaks in a constant whisper
Like the sound of an endless alarm
Only turning off when you assist Her

A simple Lady with a purpose
Her main goal is to consume you
To push out any sign of faith
She works best when it's just you two

She laughs when you are clumsy
Loving to watch you future trip
Never wanting to see you confident
Wringing out your spirit drip by drip

An owl of the night
She will never let you sleep
Being skeptical of everyone
Makes it difficult to count sheep

Quite the wealthy woman
Made her fortune off what you can't see
The unknown is what fuels her
We all know her, so who is She?

Angel of Death

When you are him, what do you see?
Is it possible for you to see the real me?
Stoic and cold, like a December night
Silence instead of text boxes, these chains are too tight

You showed me the light that had always been
I was naive for thinking you weren't like other men
Selfishness and greed, you stole my magic
If you had only stayed, I would have let you have it

For God's sake, you're just a scared little boy
You got bored and discarded me like a broken toy
Cop out after cop out, fear and shame
When I looked to you for answers, you said I was to blame

It's like drowning in the ocean and seeing dry land
Only to get there and find out it's quicksand
Or wandering in the desert and seeing an oasis
Just to discover, it was one of the Devil's many faces

Master of Disguise, you preyed on my trauma
But, you'll just tell people you didn't want the drama
"Let me see you, every single flaw"
You say I'm a child of God, yet you want to watch me crawl

A magic carpet ride that ends with disaster
Giving me hope, just to pull the rug out right after
And I know what you'll say, you'll say that you warned me.
But from where I'm standing, I see 1,000 different stories

So, go on, and take the same damn actions
But, pain and fear both lead to dissatisfaction
"Hurt people, hurt people," your favorite line
Well, "hurt people, heal themselves" is mine

You can call your people and claim harassment
But all fingers point back to your own detachment
So, walk, skip, and run away
My knees are too bruised from begging you to stay

But hey, you get what you want, you're finally alone
Make sure you take all of your things because
my vagina is not your home

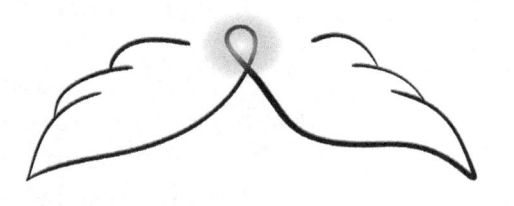

Angel of Hope

When you are him, what do you see?
Is it possible for you to see the real me?
Warm and breezy, like an April morning
Like a lighthouse, you stabilized me through the storming

You showed me the fire that had always been
No romantic feelings, I will gladly be your friend
Street lights on dark roads, you led me to my magic
It's about time I let myself have it

For God's sake, you're such a hopeful little boy
No matter how great your pain, all you spread is joy
Mistake after mistake, learning and growing
You changed my whole life without even knowing

It's like walking outside after a tornado
Just to look up at the sky and see a big rainbow
Or falling overboard when the boat tips over
Just to discover, it's easier to swim when you're sober

Student of vulnerability, you saw my trauma
Where other people failed, you invited no drama
"Let me see you, every single flaw"
I'm a child of God, it was my choice to crawl

A magic carpet ride filled with adventure
Letting the best things go is the ultimate surrender
I'm not sure what you'll say because that's not for me
From where I'm standing, we wrote one great short story

So, go on, live your truth and take your actions
My only hope is that you find great satisfaction
"Hurt people, hurt people" your favorite line
It will be "healed people, heal people" in only a matter of time

Please call your people and process my harassment
There's no excuse for my actions, despite your detachment
So, walk, skip, and run towards your healing
I'll pray for your journey, knees bruised from the kneeling
But hey, we will both be okay, know you're never alone
Because in the lake that's my heart, you, my rock, have a home

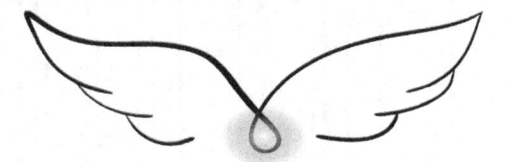

HOUSE OF LIES

House of Lies

You said it was our safe space
You'll say anything to save face
Demonize me to give a monster grace
All your leather & you steal my lace

Would you even let me walk away?
Or just love bomb me until I stay?
Freedom from you is what I pray
Trapped in your game & forced to play

At least the coffee will keep us awake
Caffeine to berate me until I break
No pouting, in your banter I must partake
A conman can always spot a fake

The grits are always the perfect side
My knees wouldn't hurt if I just complied
Character assassination taken in stride
Another attempt, but access denied

You spared me from their living hell
But I live in yours, so it's just as well
I believe the illusion, so I'll never tell
Can't be prison, if I yearn for my cell

It all comes down to my loose skin
You stood by me through thick & thin
But, I'll cut you deep with my sharp chin
I know too much, you can't let me win

There's loneliness in your big, brown eyes
Birds leave the tree for the endless skies
I look forward to the day I break your ties
Until then, I'll meet you at our House of Lies

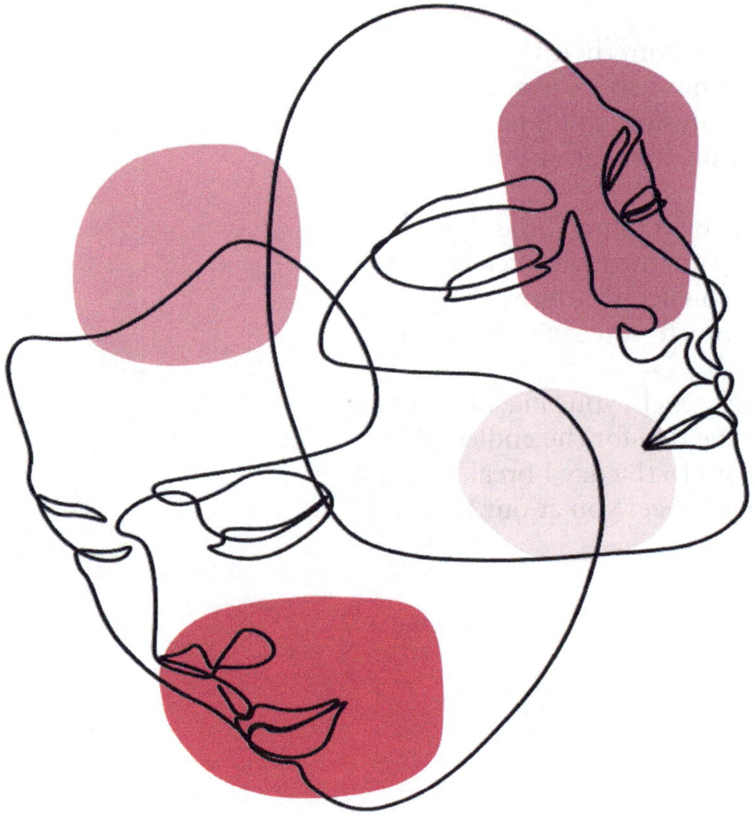

Imposter

Wake up
Smile
Laugh and breathe
When life felt lifey
You matched it with peace

We were
Oceans and rivers
Mountains and beaches
Strong connection over
Our past human leeches

Invigorating
Unnatural
To be seen and accepted
If only I had known
An imposter went undetected

Sex
Smooches
And everything in between
Broke down my walls
Wiped my cautions clean

Security
Safety
Open lines of communication

You and me together
No possibility of devastation

Texting
Calling
Saying all the right things
I sure miss the times
When my heart skipped a beat

4th of
July
Couldn't ask for better weather
Let's go to this party
And hate people together

Sausage
Fireworks
We got neither of these
Let's sneak away
"Will you go with me?"

CUE
the
RAIN
Let's switch it up &
Baffle your brain

Imposter, imposter
What do you see?
I see a happy girl
Staring back at me

Imposter, imposter
What is your plan then?
I will detach
With no rhyme or reason

Imposter, imposter
Will he come back again?
I cannot tell you
That's his decision

Imposter, imposter
How does it end?
I will destroy him
Her, collateral damage

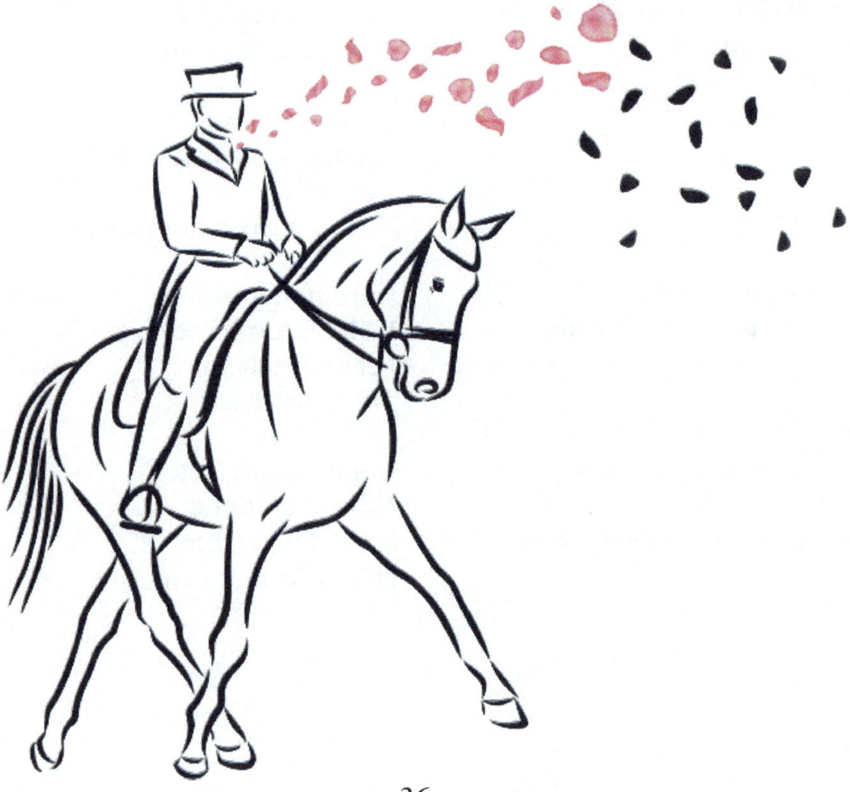

Hypocrite

The words he speaks sound so sweet
When he rides on his high horse
His inevitable dismount turns sweet to bitter
Justifying his actions with no remorse

In his town of logic and reason
Of eggshells the roads are paved
While cracks are formed at her every mistake
His misconduct is a street parade

A volcano of grandiosity and pride
He's quite impressed with his moral codes
No awareness of a double standard
Any accountability, and he'd explode

Laying out all her cards on the table
He invalidates her every feeling
But, when the bets on him
He claims it wasn't his turn dealing

A story as old as time
He fed her dinner, then got her naked
Saying he'd never do what was done to him
Well, he sure can dish it, but he can't take it

He always seems to know the answers
Even convinced her to pay his steep price
But, there are no refunds trusting a conman
An advisor that can't take his own advice

Can it really be a lost investment?
Everything he presented was illegitimate
Happy to pay for her peace of mind
She'd drain her accounts to get rid of that hypocrite

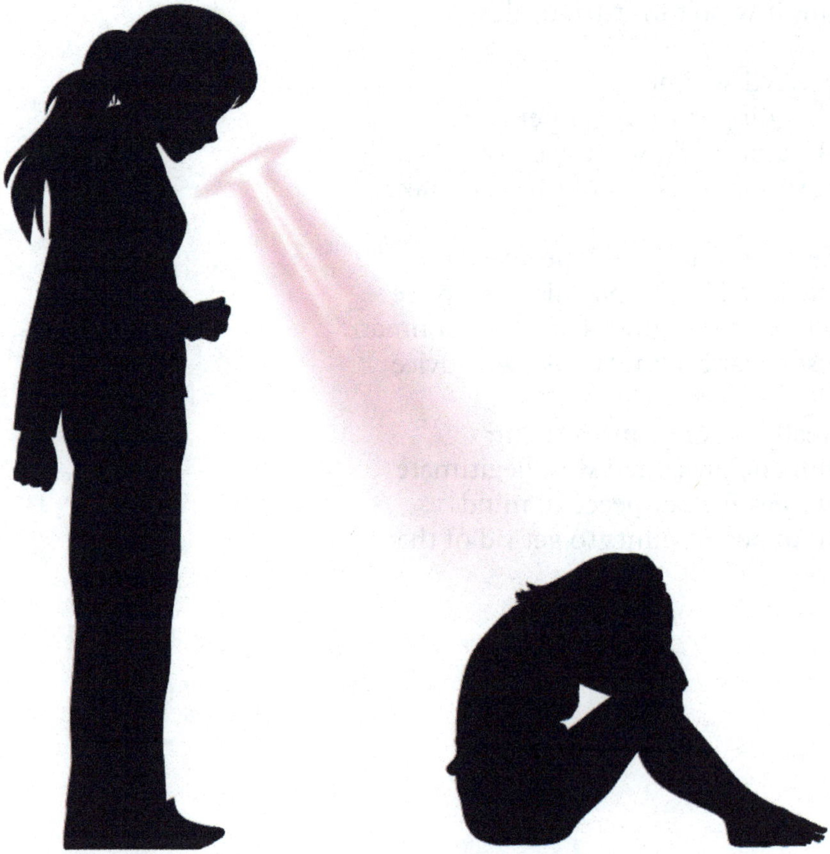

The Bigger Person

I'm always the one being held accountable
No validation, my troubles are surmountable
They tell me to reflect on my actions
And keep getting away with their infractions

Their deflection, projection, redirection
Is literally abuse, stop calling it protection
The whole love bombing/stonewalling cycle
Is psychological torture & makes people suicidal

I'm codependent, easily attached & intense
But, abuse is abuse, my trauma can't be their defense
And just because I'm the common thread
Doesn't negate that they're all intentionally messing with my head

It's been engrained to take ownership and not be the victim
Like even though he pursued me, I still picked him
Or these people that treated me less than human
Treated me how I taught them pardoning their intrusion

Y'all seriously need to stop the victim blaming
I'm not avoiding red flags, people aren't who they're claiming
My whole life I've been authentic and real
And people lie to my face, their true feelings they conceal

I love my people with a love that is unmatched
I accepted it before, but now I have completely detached
I have been disappointed by every single one of my friends
Not showing up for me, yet I call to make the amends

I have always tried to forgive them of their trespasses
I'll still forgive, but they'll forever be denied access
To say I have trust issues is an understatement
They took my magic, so they caused this "love abatement"

Terrified of being alone, I always surrendered
This time, I broke, and there's nothing to be rendered
Taking accountability before just made my life worsen
So, shrinking myself like they told me to, I can't be the bigger person

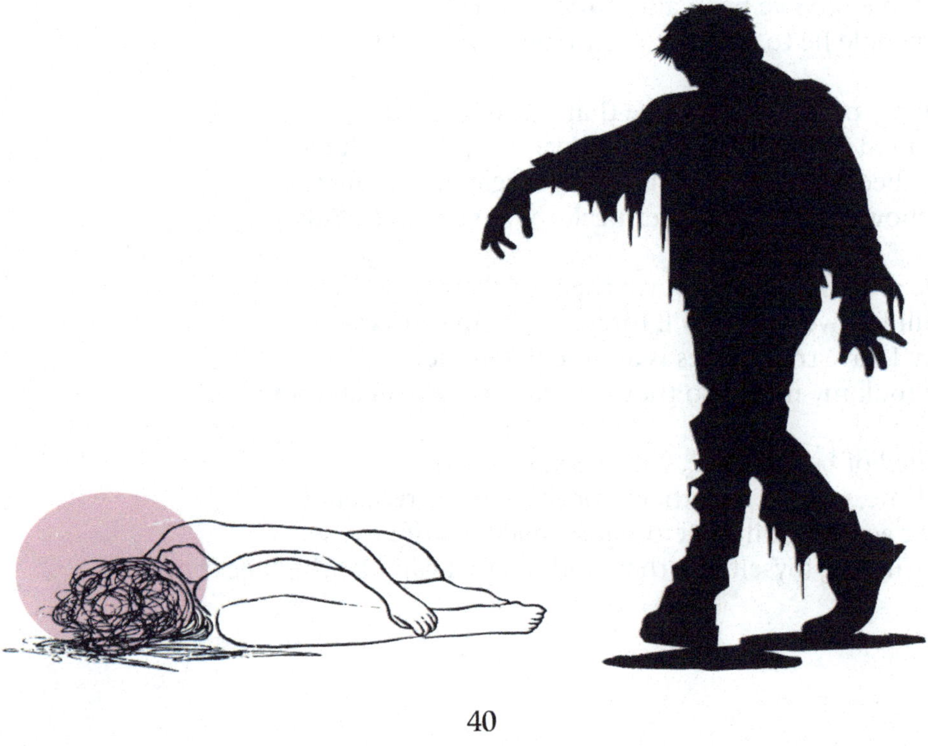

Human Monster

He's not under, but in your bed
A killer that stabs your spirit dead
Bloodied crime scene in your head
Warrant filed, must have fled

He builds love bombs, then withdraws
Attacks your kindness without cause
Men have hands, but he has claws
You bleed out, he hides the gauze

You're the peasant, and he's your King
He'll slit your throat, then make you sing
Tell you to chill, you're just a fling
Only ring he'll give you is suffering

The Gaslight Guru, you'll feel crazy
All the conversations becoming hazy
Unemployed, but you're being lazy
Giant palm tree, and you're acting shady

His favorite weapon is confusion
Locks you in his prison of delusion
No audience, he prefers seclusion
Body aside, that man's not human

But, what does it have to cost her?
Her peace and happiness forever squandered
Living nightmare, he'll always haunt her
I'd fund the hit if I knew a mobster
We need a supernatural first responder
They live among us, these human monsters

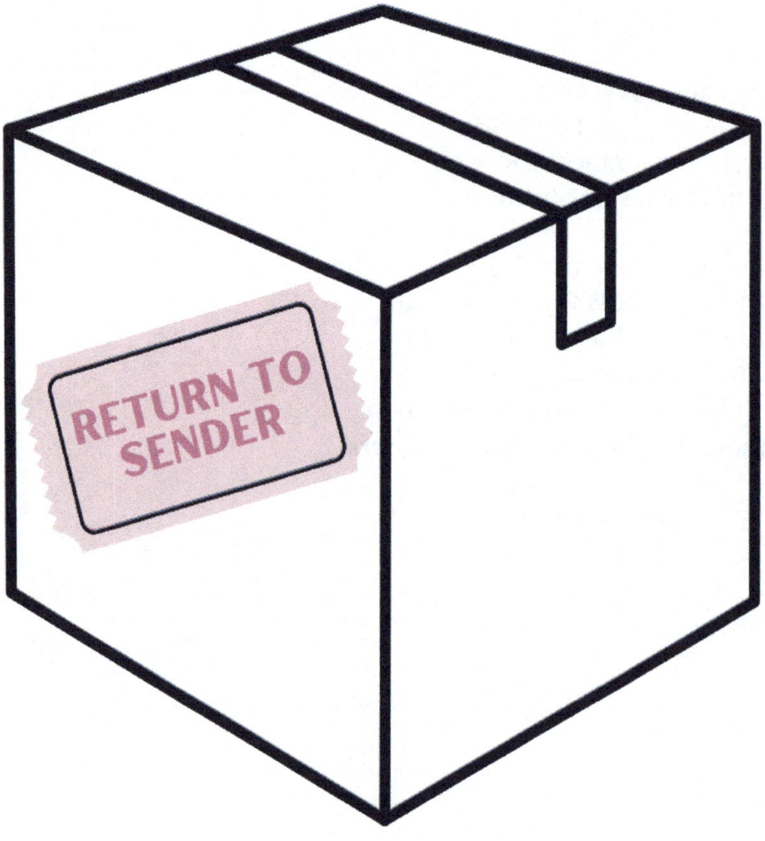
RETURN TO
SENDER

Return to Sender

You built me up and tore me down
You would never leave- Now, not a sound
You fabricated every precious memory
You dreamed that for your disease, I was your remedy

You saw and accepted all of my being
You bullied me to stay, so I could watch you fleeing
You gutted my humanity out of spite
You left me in your dark cave and stole my light

You labeled my reality as delusion
You then shamed me for my confusion
You stripped me of the joy she stripped from you
You tried to play God with your Deja Vu

You bought into the notion that misery loves company
You passed your pain like hot potato, you held the incumbency
You left me for dead with your contagious disease
You are now cured, not even a sneeze

You broke free from her torture chamber
You built one for me, and then tried to blame her
You think you're selfless wanting me to be okay
You know that's a joke because you're the source of my decay

You have thrown my iron train completely off the track
You think that just acknowledging my existence will put it back
You built a bomb of pain and mailed it to my address
You waited for my explosion, but that was a bad guess

This pain is not mine, so it will no longer be rendered
You should check for a package that says "return to sender"

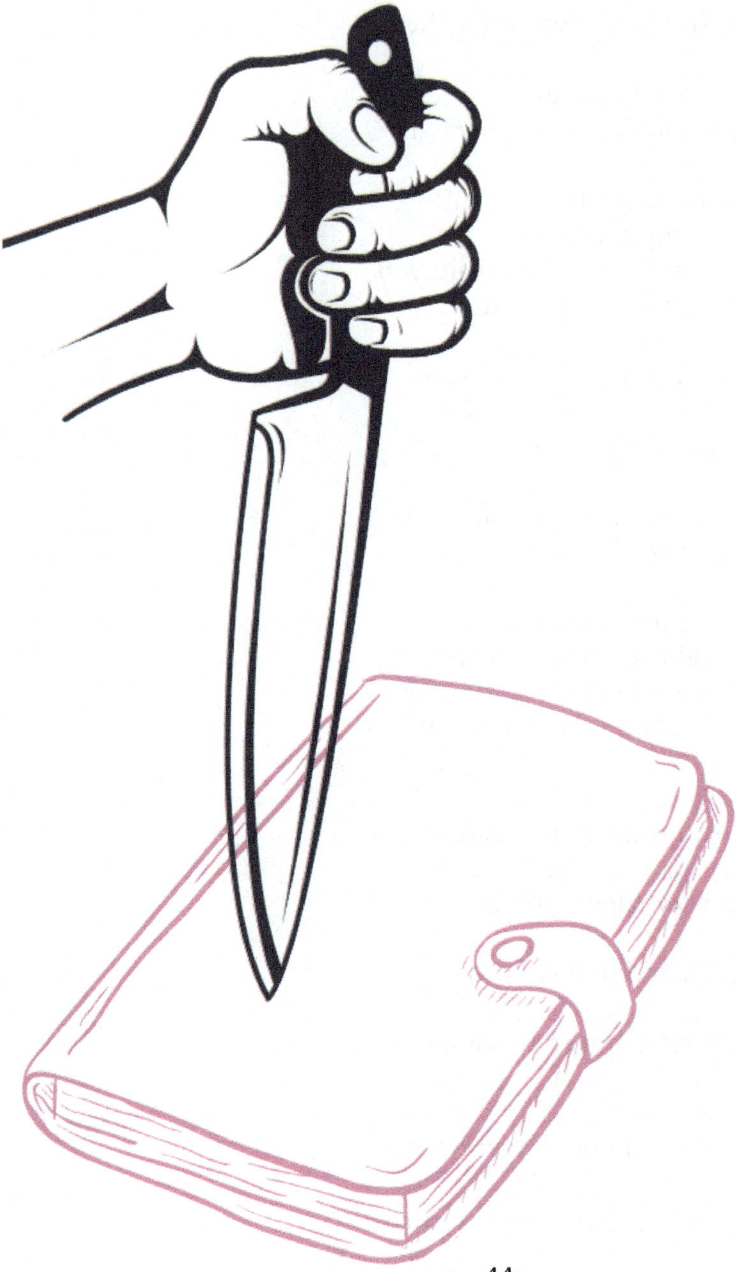

Human Diary

Filled my pages with their souls
As if my one purpose is to console

Words of heartbreak and celebration
My lack of voice yields their lack of consideration

Only want me when they need me
Dreams and wishes, their personal genie

Cut me open and bleed me dry
Then wealthy off attention when I die

Unrealistic goals and empty promises
There's no leaving, they have me in harnesses

When they're done, they'll just discard me
If they want a new one, they'll get a carbon copy

They're my priority, while I'm their option
If I was worth money, they'd put me up for auction

Their venting constructs a double standard
My pages have lines, I must stay well-mannered

They all admire my shoe collection
Must've walked a mile in them with all their corrections

They know I'll never run out of space
From pen to pencil- my truth they will erase

Angry words, they trade pencil for knife
Stab me in the back, but bring a bag of ice

Them as pots and me their kettle
They say their black ink is just coincidental

Unsolicited, doesn't stop their advisory
Favorite tip is to suggest me psychiatry
Condescending, concerned about my sobriety
Leave them on read, they just start using bribery
Self-made critics, all they offer is anxiety
If they keep it up, they'll all lose me entirely
Unoriginal, why can't they add some variety
Bullies should remember a corpse can't respond to inquiries

So, forget your happy friends
How about you check on your human diaries?

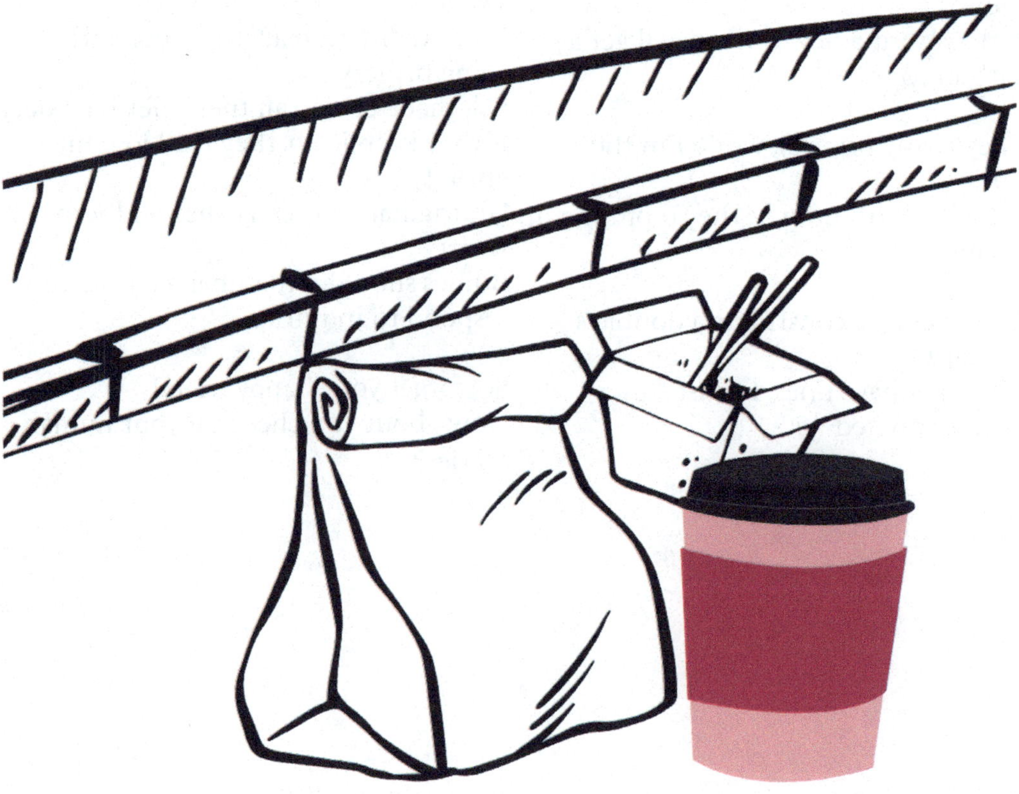

Empty Parking Lot

How many endless conversations
Have we had at multiple locations
Never seeming to have a final destination
Always leaving me in total devastation

Time feels like an illusion
But, you live in a delusion
Never coming to a conclusion
I just want to find a solution

There's always a logical explanation
Gaslighting my need for contemplation
You were the one wanting open communication
But, this has become a one-sided conversation

Treating me less than human
You like to shame my confusion
Being me has become an intrusion
I'll check myself into an institution

Words cryptic and begging for interpretation
Steal my magic like a game of exploitation
Showed me who you are then ridiculed my expectation
Give me an inch just to spend a mile in hesitation

Depressed only wanting seclusion
Not the same after your persecution
Soon, you'll just find a substitution
Call the guard, I'm ready for my execution

Emotional hemophilia, this sadness won't clot
Memories of us that you easily forgot
There is something deep inside me beginning to rot
Just like unwanted leftovers in an empty parking lot

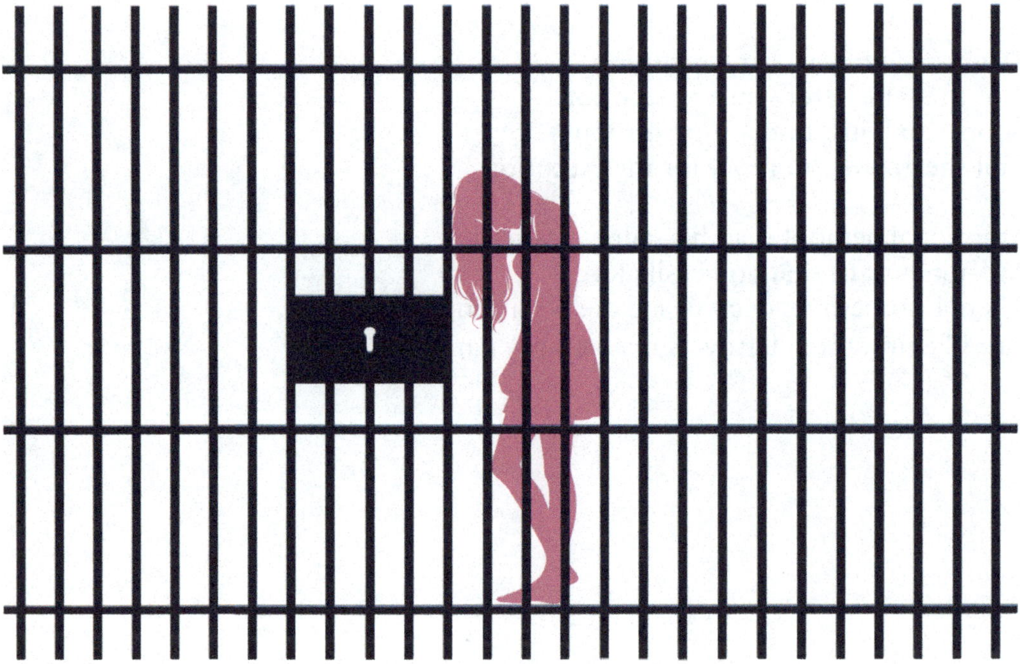

Solitary Confinement

The last one was brutal, I'm not the same
It was a losing battle, just a pawn in his game
Gathered the wounded and retreated home
Details of the peace treaty are still unknown

Like a veteran must return to home life
Trying to fit what's changed just leads to strife
The girl they once knew died on the battlefield
Mistaking enemy for friend, I left my shield

A corpse with a heartbeat, I lost my spark
Others approach me, unafraid of my bark
When all I want is to be left alone
Blocked their numbers, they just use a different phone

I have nothing to give of myself anymore
When I would have given him the world before
And I don't want a damn thing from anyone else
But, they hope they'll be the one to make my frozen heart melt

I've never known how to play pretend
My fake smiles seem to only offend
Broken pieces that no one can mend
Let me put it into words you can comprehend

This new me/old life combination
Feels exactly like an incarceration
Given up on all of my manifestations
I've lost all hope of motivation
Truth is, I'm bored of this conversation
You want me out in the general population?
Well, all I want is to be in isolation
It's my one desired destination

Same act, but different scene
It's my turn to get obscene

Say it again for the people in the back
Let's keep it on track, we've got a lot to unpack
One more time, in case you didn't hear me
I'm not the same girl I once appeared to be

What she did to him, he did right back to me
Based on the cycle, I'm up for a killing spree
So, beg the warden to take it under advisement
I'm a danger to the public, I need solitary confinement

SECTiON 3: INiTiATiON

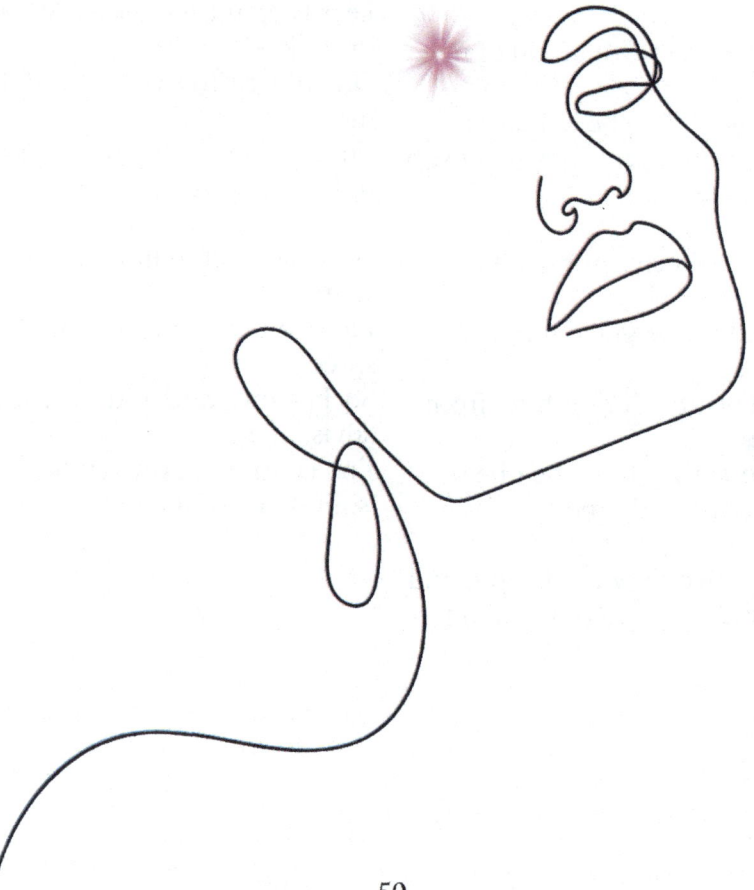

Initiation: Who is He?

It doesn't matter where you grew up
He's your friendly neighbor across the street
That always keeps His yard pristine
Even in the Summer's scorching heat

He could hear your parents fighting
When they returned from late events
But, He never meddled in their business
He'd just lend an ear if they needed to vent

Not quite sure what He did for work
But, rumor has it, He made serious money
Although, you would never be able to tell
He drove around in an old Punch Buggy

There was that time at the Fall Festival
He was honored for His years of volunteering
His face turned bright red like a tomato
Must've been embarrassed from all the cheering

And at all the neighborhood block parties
He'd bring cupcakes- His famous was carrot
The women always fawned over His baking
It was His wife's recipe- He refused any credit

I actually remember the day His wife passed
It was sudden, and He didn't understand
In Springtime, when He was tending to her garden
He called us, unafraid to ask for helping hands

He has an unwavering faith in God
Like He trusts his plan to every degree
Confident and knows His place in the world
We all know Him, so who is He?

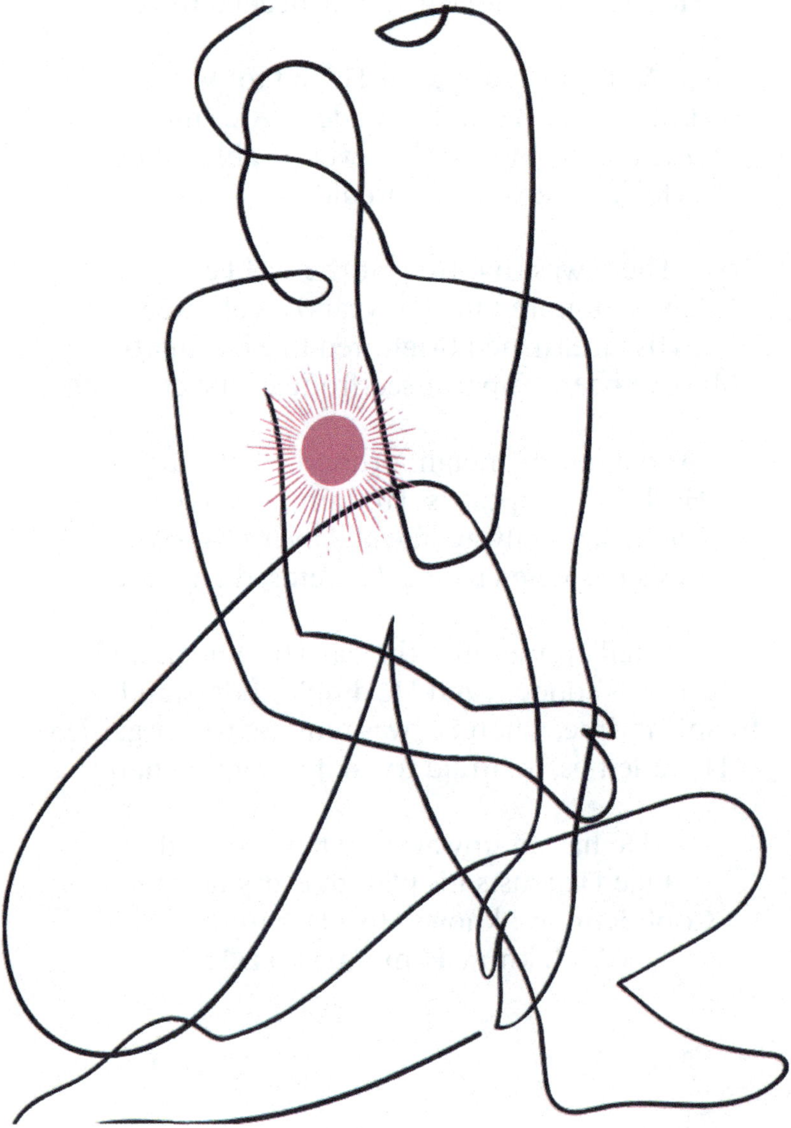

Healing

This pain is so bizarre
Cloudy sky, but a shooting star
Sharp, yet so hollow
Tell me, where do fallen tears go?

"It's just going to take some time"
Rattling in my ears like a chime
There's no way out but through
Where's the back arrow, so I can press "undo?"

Each night I dread tomorrow's anguish
Praying it will be the day my demons are finally vanquished
What a burden it is to live with that plight
When sick children are begging God for just one more night

The tears, like a river, will not stop streaming
Car talks with God, people concerned at my screaming
Run in the door and into the fetal position
Pass out from the pain, a demonic repetition

Lava of torture constantly flowing through my veins
Slave to his prison, but he's lost the key to my chains
Edge of my seat hoping to hear the profound
I guess in order to break free, I'll have to break down

I have loved
I have lost
I have felt warmth
I have felt frost
I have seen birth
I have seen death
I have wished for more time
I have wished for my last breath
I have cried for God
I have cried for him
I have shined like the Sun
I have watched my light dim
I have an ache in my heart that will never go away
I have a love in my heart that will permanently stay

There's nothing I can do to escape the feeling
Better accept my hand, God is done dealing
Begged for the why, answers He's not revealing
Praying every day, knees sore from the kneeling
Pain not relieved, prayers bouncing off the ceiling
Red-faced and snot-nosed, face unappealing
Angry and selfish, the ugly I'm no longer concealing
Put it all out in the open, this is the reality of healing

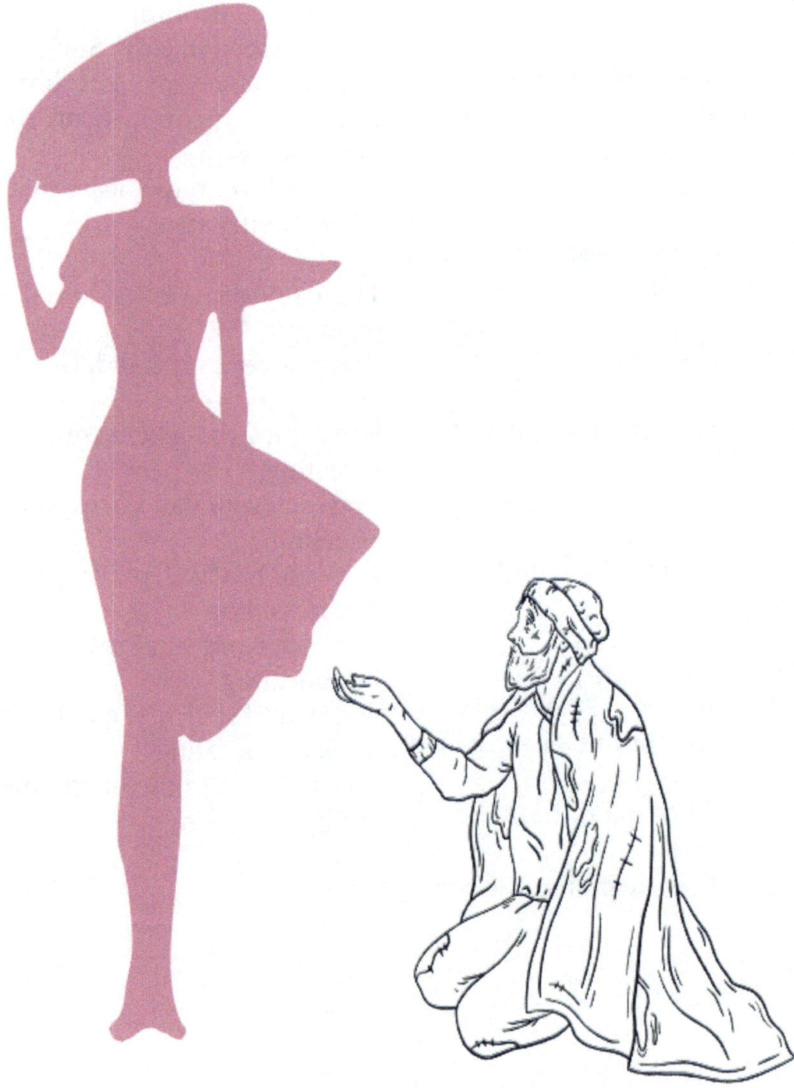

Becoming

Staying in this place hurts
Mistakenly, I believed leaving it behind
Would somehow feel worse

I keep looking to others for the answer
Even though it's impossible for them
To treat my emotional cancer

I've begged God to remove the pain
This time He is preoccupied and
His silence means the agony will remain

Well, I guess I need to choose my hard
I've been forcing "love" with a man who
Found me extremely easy to discard

Afraid to connect with a new soul
I've been living in the past thinking
Those dead relationships are what will make me whole

But, in this place no new life can grow
It's been a nice intermission, now it's time to
Get on with the rest of the show

If I walk away, I will never look back
He probably thinks I will because
Each time before I'd always crack

I've spent my time as the damsel in distress
This isn't an outdated fairytale so
I have to take ownership of my own success

It's true that what he did to me was tragic
But at least when he blew us up in flames it
Reignited my magic

He may have feelings, but he'll still cower
He wasn't the first deceiving thief to
Try and steal my motherfucking power

To his sick abuse I am no longer succumbing
So, he can watch me glow up and
Grovel at the feet of the woman I am becoming

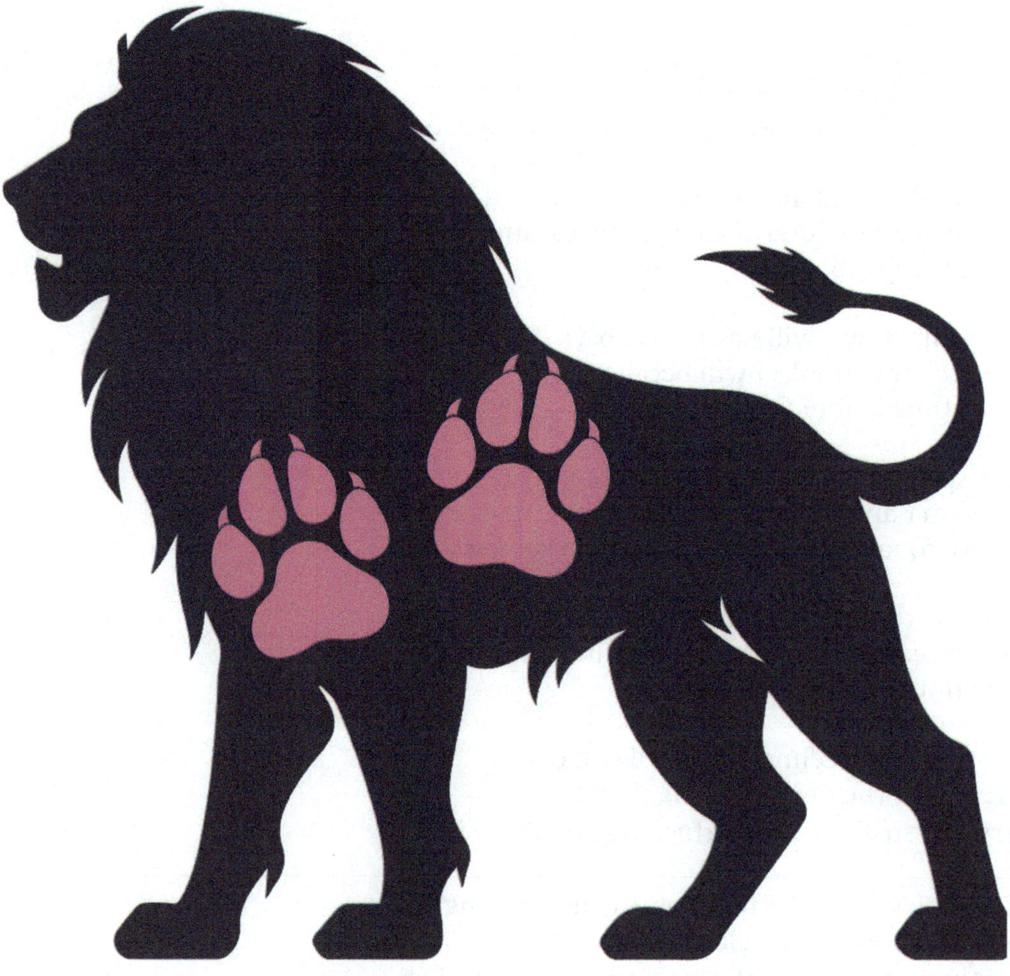

Claws

They kicked her while she was down
No life jacket, they let her drown
Only seeing her weakness
Just a scared attempt to muzzle her uniqueness

Told her to change who she was at her core
Invited a shame spiral like never before
Repulsed by her reflection every single day
Can it really be a hunt chasing such easy prey?

Odd man out, she started to believe it
Stole her light for a chance at her wit
Well, candles eventually stop burning
But, just like the sun rise, hers is forever returning

She began to see right through their lies
That they kept her down out of fear she would rise
Always knowing she possessed a magic
They only tortured her because they didn't have it

While they were busy magnifying her flaws
She was tucked away & sharpening her claws

She is a lioness
Fierce and Bright
Here is her Pain
Oh, but here is her Light
When She lets her wild out
Hear Her Might
So, fall to your knees & pray She won't Bite

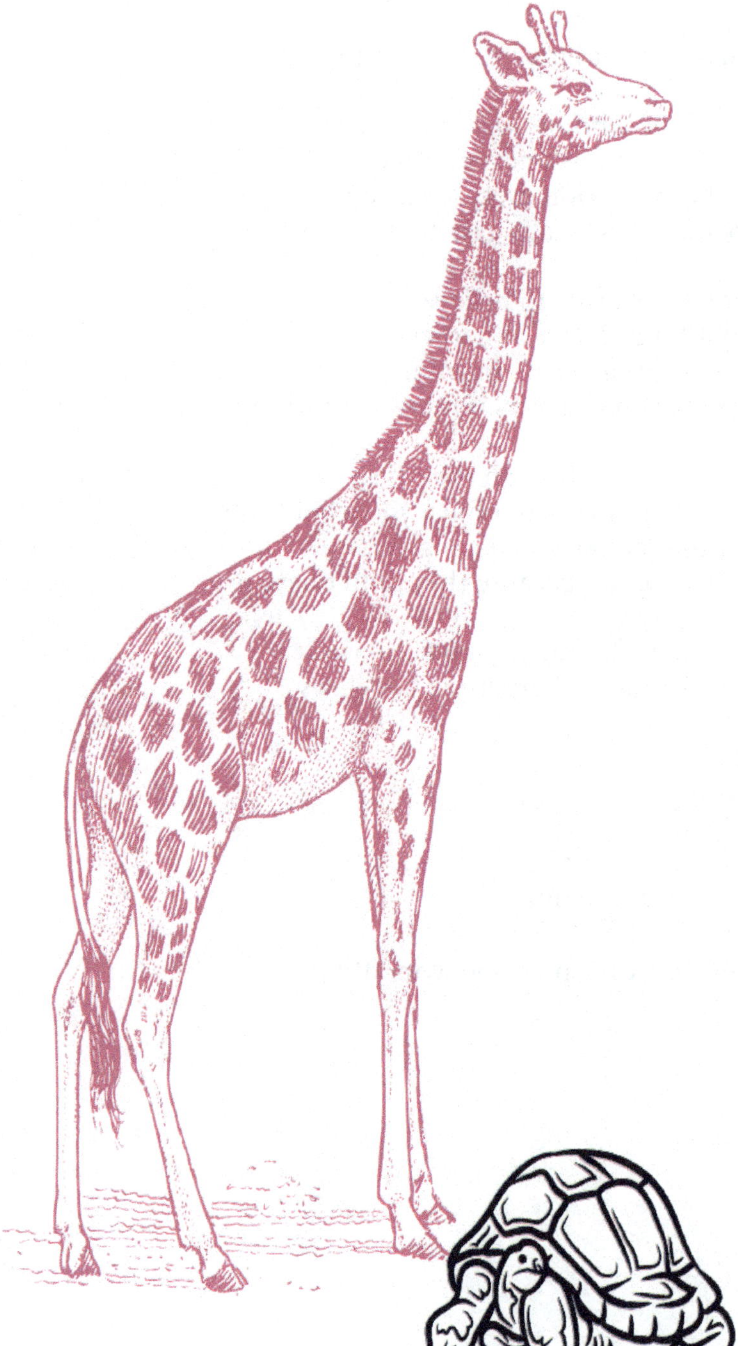

Giraffe

My favorite animal is the giraffe
I thought it symbolized my other half

On the surface, me and that creature
Seem to have completely opposite features

The giraffe stands tall, but hustles in silence
I am a mere 5"2, the drama's been my reliance

Above it all, the giraffe embodies grace
Looking down on me, I've let others tell me my place

Standing alone, I now see it clearly
Others misguided me out of fear - I mean that sincerely

Metaphorically, I have a Giraffe's vision
My intuition and insight let me see with precision

The giraffe stands tall and can see above the rest
Although, I am short, I can infer what you suggest

A giraffe's height allows him to see for miles
A turtle standing next to him would just scoff in denial

But, the turtle can never have that perspective
He will always believe the Giraffe's vision is defective

Meanwhile, the turtle will be scolding our tall friend
With his long neck, to hear the turtle, he will have to bend

Bending too long and listening to lies
Can cut off his oxygen, the giraffe can even die

I am a giraffe with vision clear as crystal
Gaslighting what I see, turtles I've let belittle

Bending my neck to hear their cruel words
I almost lost my breath, but an intuition occurred

These turtles will never see the perspective I've been granted
Everything they tell me will always be turtle slanted

So, I can stand tall and know what I see is true
And the turtles can try to convince me I'm wrong like turtles do

But, I will remember that I am a long-necked giraffe
And turtles will always need my vision to see on their behalf

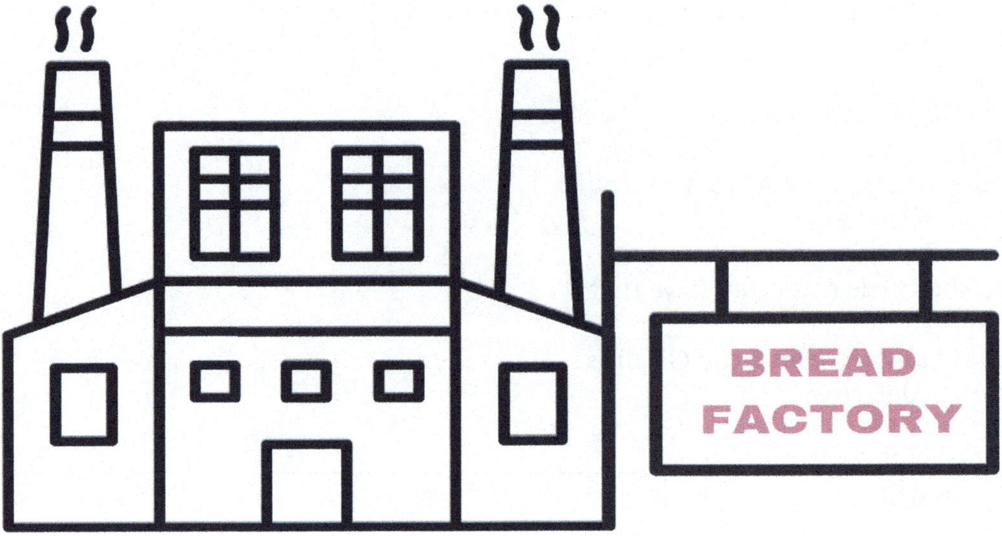
BREAD
FACTORY

Breadcrumbs

Men can't be witches - the world's oldest lie
The wart's not on your nose, it's in your left eye
You make herbal potions and cast wordy spells
Even have flying monkeys that defend you so well

You remind me of the witch from Hansel and Gretel
For a remote cabin in the woods, you'd gladly resettle
You used the same ploy as the witch in that tale
Throwing breadcrumbs to control me in the form of a trail

I was alone in the woods at the point of starvation
Your inconsistent breadcrumbs conditioned salivation
Always frantically looking for your next tiny scrap
It became a game of survival, I didn't see your trap

Selfish and evil, always wanting to take
You fabricated love, and she baited with cake
Both of you taking advantage of innocence
She dangled sweets, you weaponized ambivalence

You left me in the woods, your trail running dry
After everything we went through, you can't even reply
When the conversation grew cold, I built my own fire
The light uncovered a way out I hadn't see prior

When we first met, you made many false claims
As they were discovered, you gaslit me with blame
I'm no longer confused & your breadcrumbs aren't satisfactory
I don't want your slice or your loaf - I'm building my own bread factory

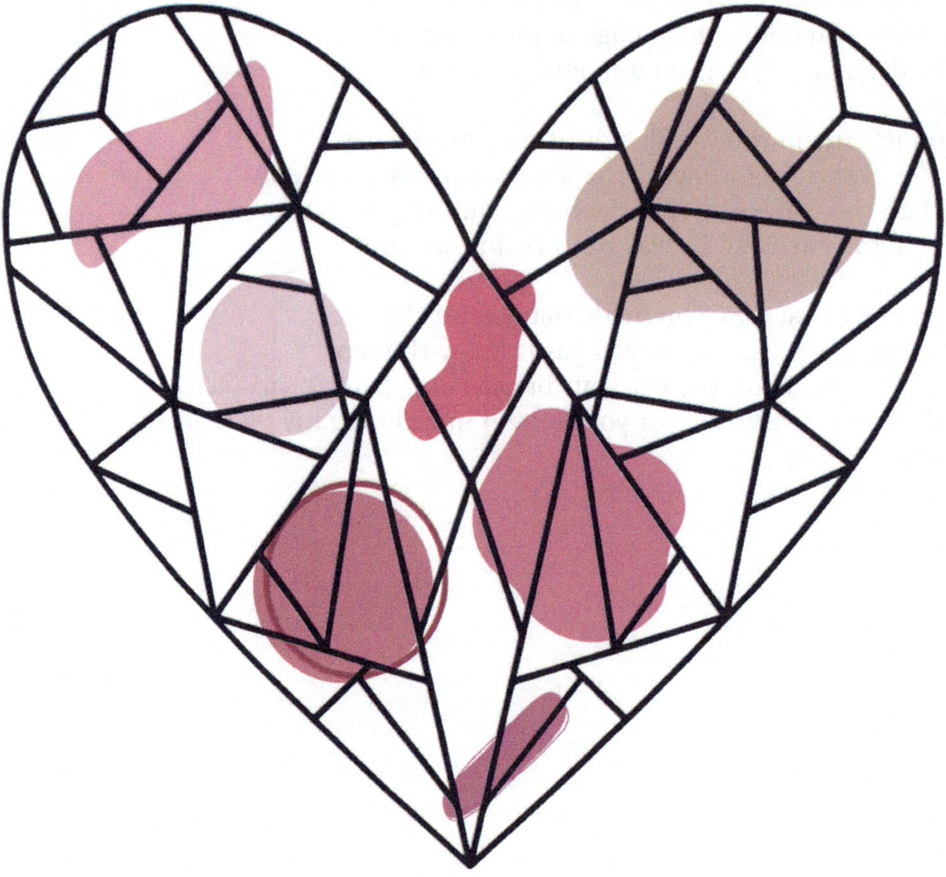

Home

With her Motherland in chaos
My heart was forced to seek asylum
Finding refuge in neighboring countries
A false stability traded for my love

So, the fragments of my heart
Were dispersed across the globe
Creating a fatal and empty void
Feeling relief only when they were close

For years, I believed I was a citizen
When it turns out, I had been illegal
Though I proudly sang their anthems
Each deportation became more lethal

In detainment, the truth was blinding
Their corruption could not evade me
When you pledge allegiance to delusion
You only risk your emotional safety

If home is where the heart is
It's no wonder I've been homeless
With a "For Sale" sign on my forehead
The loss of dignity was my signing bonus

But, at all the open houses
I entertained unavailable buyers
It taught me how to sort them out
No more "Free Refreshments" on my fliers

Each of my heart shards they threw back
Had me out for days, in bed I would lay sick
But, now I've picked up all of the pieces
There's something beautiful about mosaics

She's travelled around the world
My heart's most loved when we're alone
So, if home is where the heart is
Well, I guess, I better make myself at home

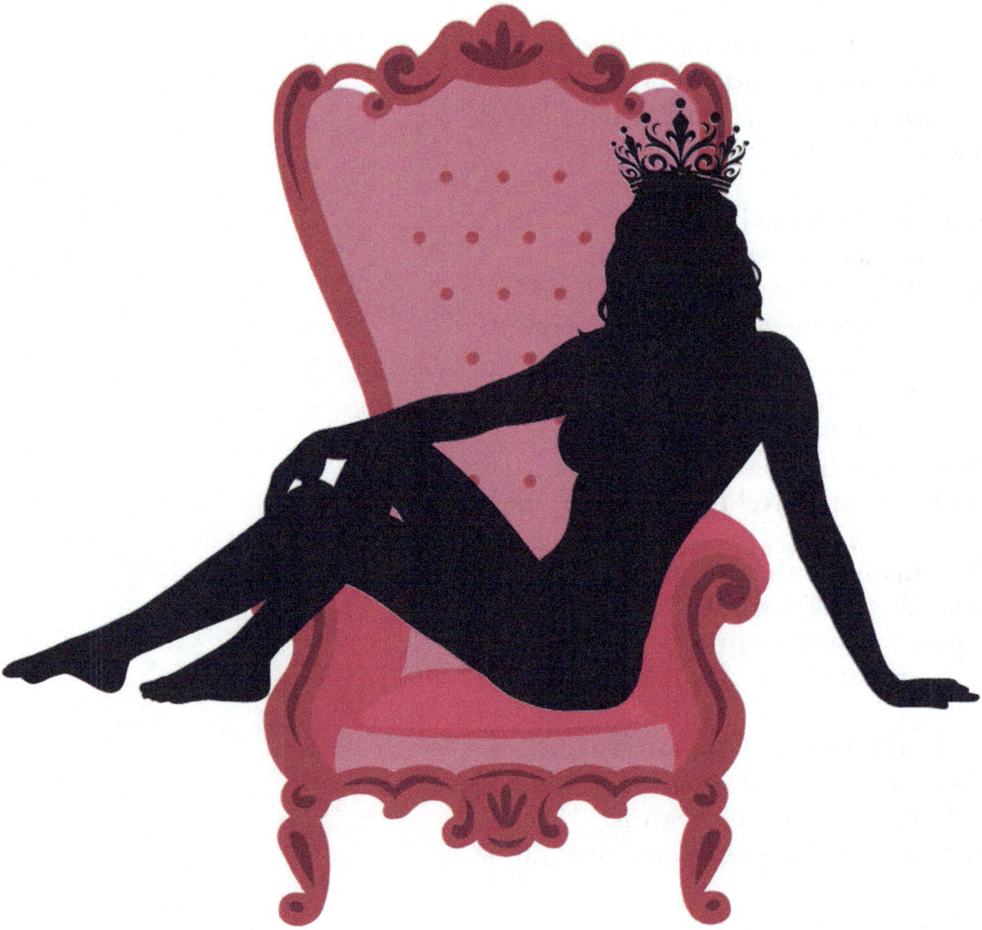

She is

She is broken, hopeless, lost and defeated
She is bloodied, battered, bruised and depleted

She is trial & error, fake smiles, and all pretend
She is living in the past, wishing for yesterdays, wanting it all again

She is be a better woman, daughter, sister & friend
She is give more, empty your cup, this time break don't bend

She is too much, overly sensitive, intense and extreme
She is controlling, always in her will, selfish, but with no self-esteem

She is wake up crying, no more joy, and I can't do this anymore
But, wait a second
She is also, I have been here before

She is strength, resilience, a woman made of stone
She is heart of gold, soul of magic, a majestic queen on her throne

She is the water, the earth, the wind and the fire
She is 100 paintings, 1,000 poems, and 10,000 songs of a choir

She is the northern star, an intricate snowflake with the vastness of the ocean
She is fairy dust, mystical, Hope matched with Devotion

She is wild horses, pouring rain, he doesn't love me - breaking free
She is the Sun rise, the morning birds, the new day - she is me

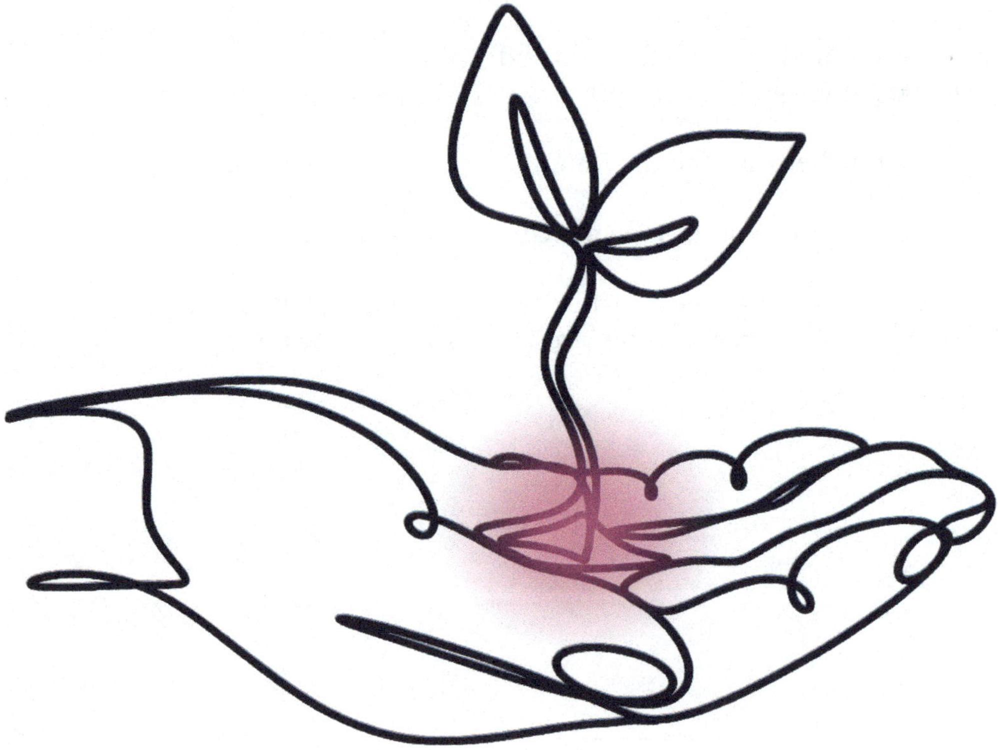

Buried Alive

Stare in my eyes while you dig my grave
It wouldn't end this way if I'd just behave
Find someone better like you truly believe
So, shovel the dirt until I can't breathe

This is what I get for seeing the real you
Have to bury me away before I leave too
Quite the paradox, killing me to keep me
Afraid with the choice, I'd choose to be free

How is it so easy for you to walk away?
When our story was written, even had a screenplay
Now, I'm just another old skeleton in your closet
Pain was inevitable, although I tried to not cause it

Well, I've been gifted with a change of perspective
I've thought your rejection meant that I am defective
My oxygen decreasing, losing sight of the miracle
Better calm myself before I get hysterical

I'll put it in words you can understand
Imagine holding a tiny seed in your hand
Place it in the earth to witness its growth
With sunshine and water, it becomes a lifelong oath

I am the seed you think you are burying
Roots and flowers my soul had been carrying
Angry at God, believing my prayers went ungranted
The beauty is, I'm not being buried, I'm being planted

In darkness, it seems the horizon only brings doom
Embrace the darkness, not buried, just planted. So, bloom.

Shedding

Every summer, I get sunburned without fail
Talk myself out of sunscreen, despite my skin being pale
The Sun is powerful, so the burn bubbles with Her rage
It hurts to move, now my flesh has become my cage

My clothes rub against my skin causing immense pain
The heat radiating from my body feels like an acid rain
But, at night I get so cold, I actually start to shiver
The fever is inevitable, nothing can stop the quiver

I try to hide the red, but everyone can see
Even the most expensive make-up can't hide burns that are third degree
Looking down from their high horses, the view is always better
It's the perfect vantage point to inspect my scarlet letter

No matter what I do, I cannot feel comfort
Thought I could trade my supply of endless tears and walk away triumphant
But, this summer was scorching, the evidence left on my skin
Unlike years prior, come Autumn my healing process did not yet begin

Every day, I still hurt and cry from the burning
Just a moment of relief is for what I am yearning
Each time I think I can see the light at the end
It's just another train in the tunnel sending me deeper within

Last night, I wanted to give up and throw it all away
But, the burn, herself, sizzled "just wait another day"
This morning when I woke, the anguish I was dreading
On my bed was a flake of skin- it's finally here - my shedding

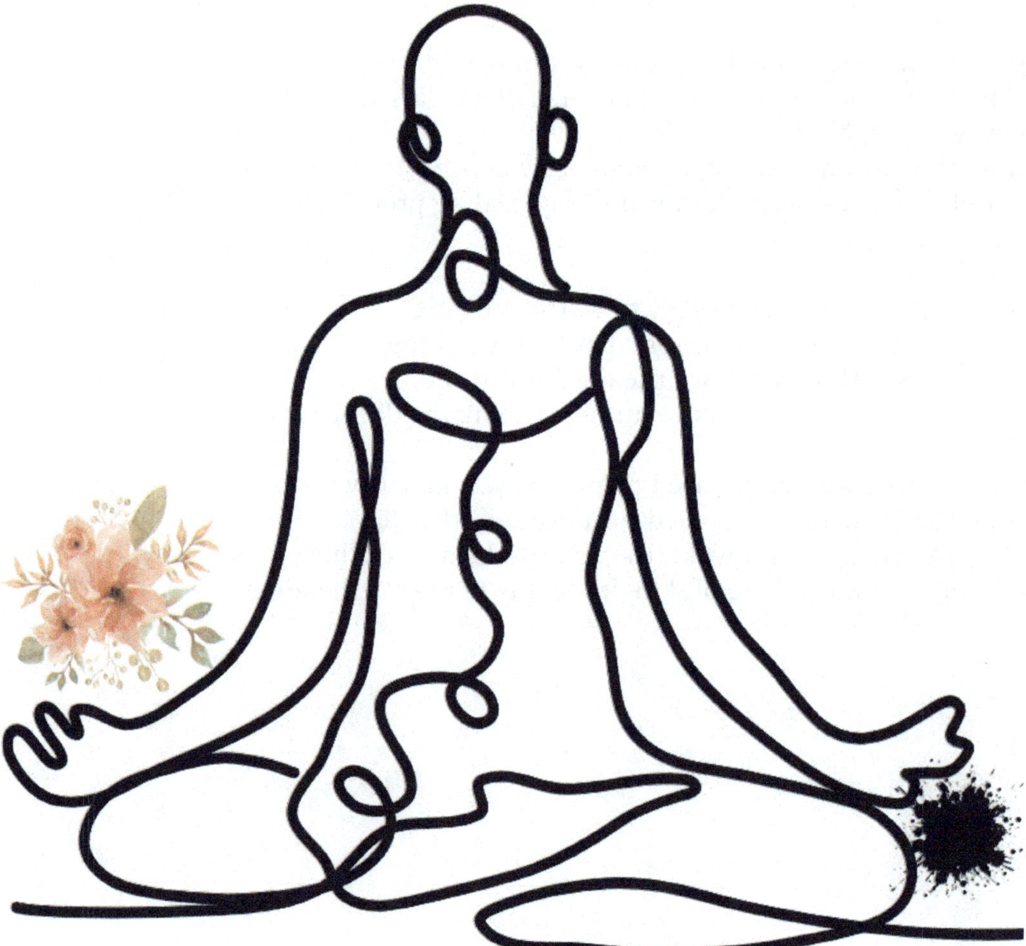

The Gain

If pain is promised, and suffering is a choice
I am just the victim of my inner voice
If a miracle is a simple change in perception
My bad luck has been of my own deception

Fired from a job and missing all purpose
Just to find your career, and it all being worth it
Losing a loved one to a deadly disease
But, in the midst of the grief, being rich with the memories

Left broken-hearted by your one true soulmate
Then, meeting your other half and seeing it was all fate
A depression so potent you start decomposing
But, soil mixed with compost is how life starts growing

Every Winter it's difficult to see beyond the cold
But, Spring always returns with her colors so bold
Each mistake that places your sanity in question
Starts to make sense when you see the greater lesson

In our troubles, we tend to miss the silver linings
But, it all comes down to God's ultimate designing
I've been choosing to suffer, the peace I'm declining
My outlook on pain, I will be redefining
The truth is there's something we should all be combining

If you face your 'pain' but lose the 'p'
Combine it with gratitude by adding the 'g'

There is nothing we can do to avoid the pain
But, if you practice gratitude, you can find the gain

SECTION 4: NiRVANA

Nirvana: Who is He?

He probably wasn't in your class
But, He went to all of our schools
Diagnosed with cancer at eleven
Each day was like His precious Jewel

The day He had his head shaved
He was confident and making jokes
Never saw Him shed a tear
His courage brought us all hope

He travelled to different cities
To get treatment and meet with Doctors
He not once complained of being tired
Begged his Mom to let Him play Soccer

Each time a teacher stopped Him
To ask Him how He's doing
No matter how sick he felt
He always replied, "Everyday, I'm improving!"

After His first major surgery
He was out of class for days
We brought His schoolwork to His house
He was on His knees giving God praise

And when the cancer came back
He held His parents as they cried
Reminding them of God's greater plan
With His tiny hand, their tears He dried

On the last day of His life
He was smiling, peaceful, and free
Dying without an ounce of fear in His body
We all know Him, so who is He?

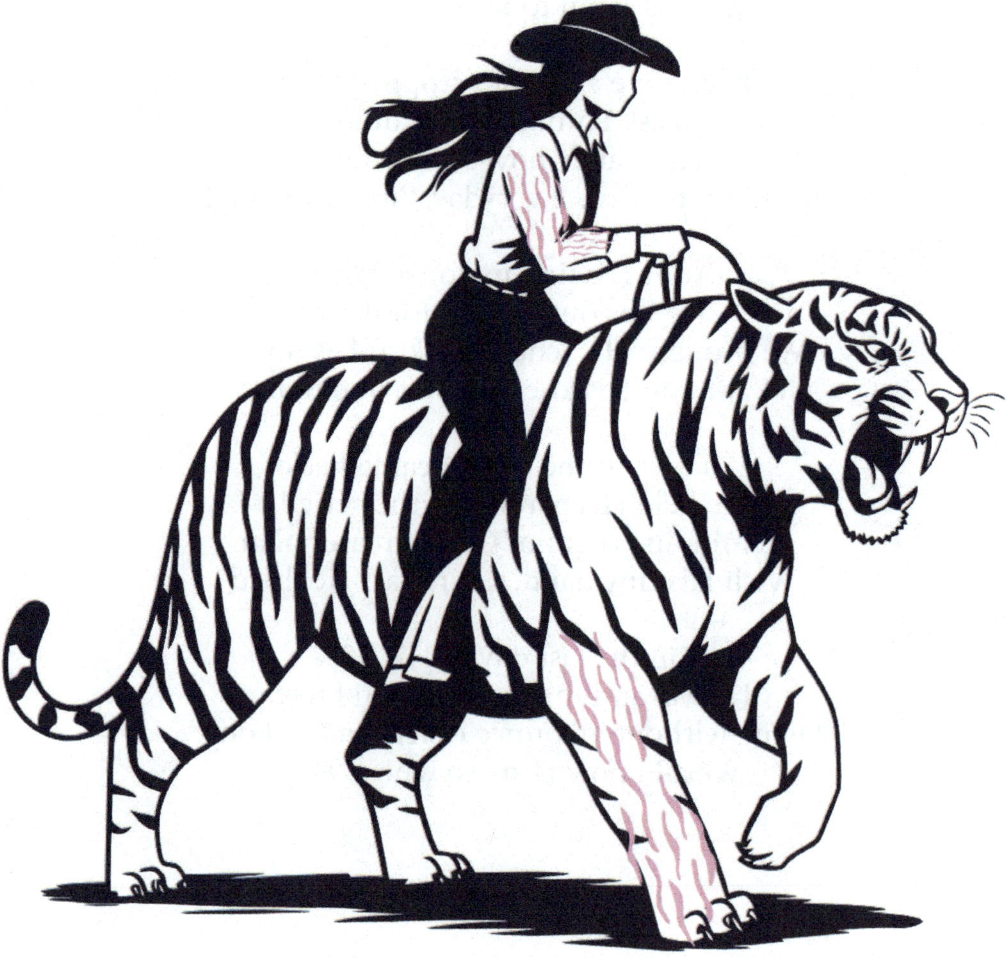

The Deep Knows

There's a group of people on this earth
That learned too early what a life is worth
They have lost their innocence way too soon
Wondering why to death they were immune

It's a subtle darkness deep in their eyes
The vault that holds their screams & cries
It can only be seen by someone who's felt it
Easy to spot, their hope has melted

They pretend to entertain your worldly problems
But, while you're talking, they turn down the volume
When you go through hell, you start to not care
Everyone feels pain, but this is despair

When they dress each morning, they wear happy faces
But, if they had the choice, with their Angels they'd switch places
What a burden it is to feel guilty for living
For the rest of their lives, they will try to master forgiving

You have to understand, they're a type of survivor
As the last one's standing, they're ranked the number one fighters
When all they really want is one last moment beside her
Shaming themselves for being unable to revive her
Spiritual stripes, they're all God's vicious tigers
Not blinded by the darkness, just made their lights shine brighter
Every mistake was another lesson that made them wiser
If you haven't been through it, you'll always be an outsider

These are soldiers that God himself chose
Like a Phoenix from the ashes, they too arose
They are steady and strong, like a river flows
Keep getting back in the ring, despite the blows
Because of their darkness, the brighter their light glows

They've had their lows
They've experienced woes

They are the people who know the Deep Knows

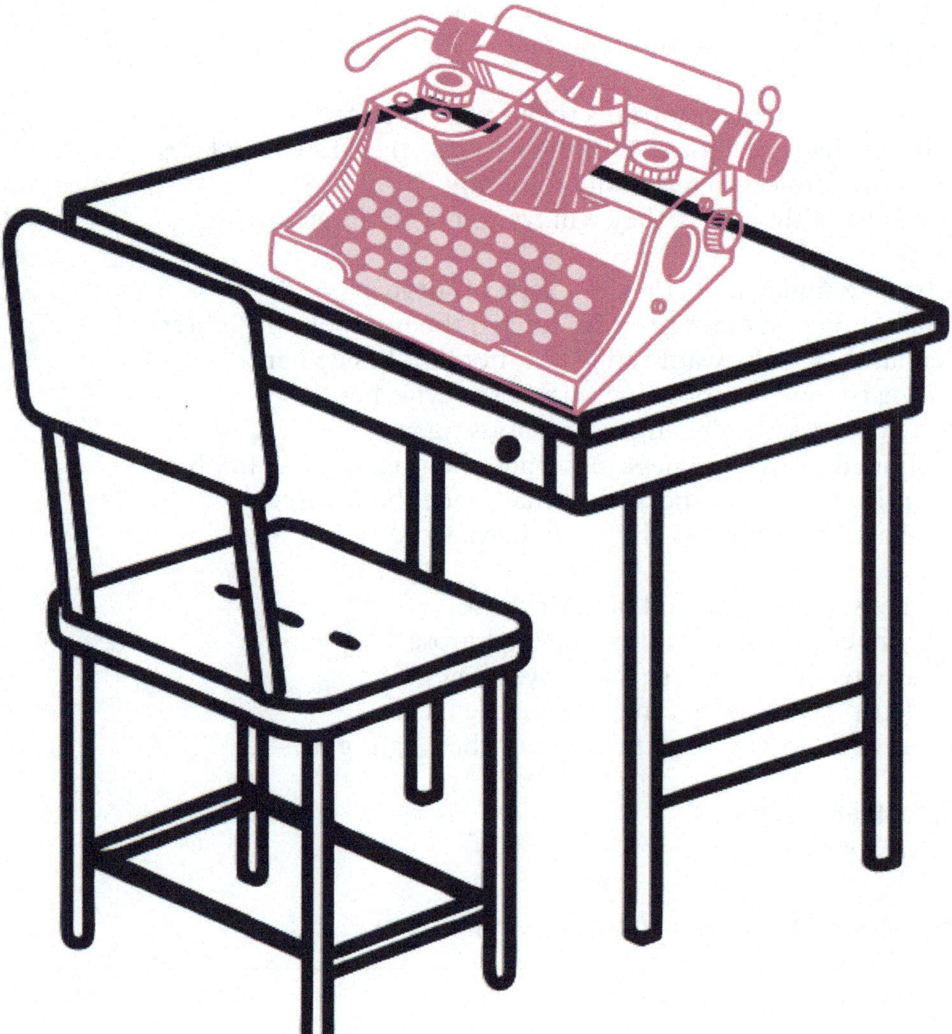

200 Ladies

Time has managed to turn thinking into work
My mind's eye employs 200 elderly, female clerks
Analyzing, assessing & luke-warm coffee
On Christmas, Joyce brings her famous English Toffee

Rapidly typing into old type writers
They smoke Virgina Slims and have monogrammed lighters
Each assigned a mission with no room to fail
They're diagnosed with OCD and have great attention to detail

You don't want Doris on story telling duty
She tends to stir the pot when she's feeling moody
And Barb plays back all past interactions
Her perfectionism guarantees the dissatisfaction
Trudy's the boss and keeps them all in line
Walks around with a yardstick that sends a shiver down your spine
Maureen is never sure and always asks questions
I think her uncertainty is somehow linked to my intestines
Gertrude is hopeful and tends to always see the bright side
Although, she is bitter her events keep getting denied
Then you have Susan, she's been here from the start
Even though she falls asleep by lunchtime, no one wants her to depart
Rose is the one they all go to for answers
Gives them all hope because she's quite the romancer
My favorite is Sandra because she always makes me laugh
She's up all day and night researching jokes on my behalf
Paula is curious and seems to always be learning
Her lack of study breaks is starting to be a bit concerning
And then there's Ann, the quiet one of the group
If you put one thing out of order, it'll send her in a loop
Alicia's face is serious and pensive
Her daily reports tend to be the most extensive
Linda deals with relationships which causes her to worry
Maybe that's why she has me over say "I'm sorry"
Bertha is grumpy and loves to be sarcastic
She'll just roll her eyes when anyone's enthusiastic

It's true my head consists of women well into their eighties
But, in any fight, I would never bet against my 200 Ladies

Arrival

I have wasted precious time
So focused on the destination
Exhausted from the planning
Never could enjoy the vacation

I started to fight life's terms
And I lost all control
I threw away weeks of my life
Gave up, crawled into my dark hole

As the big lumps of life came
Because they inevitably would
I switched on my autopilot
A robot would do better than I could

I learned that the time will always pass
If I'm in the darkness or in the sun
And letting others determine my happiness
Are choices that can never be undone

If life is a pot of boiling water
I have a difficult choice to make
I can be a potato and soften
Or harden like an egg with a shell to break

I choose to be a potato
Growing softer as the heat rises
With no outer shell to harden me
I can celebrate life & all her surprises

There's a beauty that comes naturally
When you stop living for survival
It was only when I embraced the journey
That I could truly appreciate the arrival

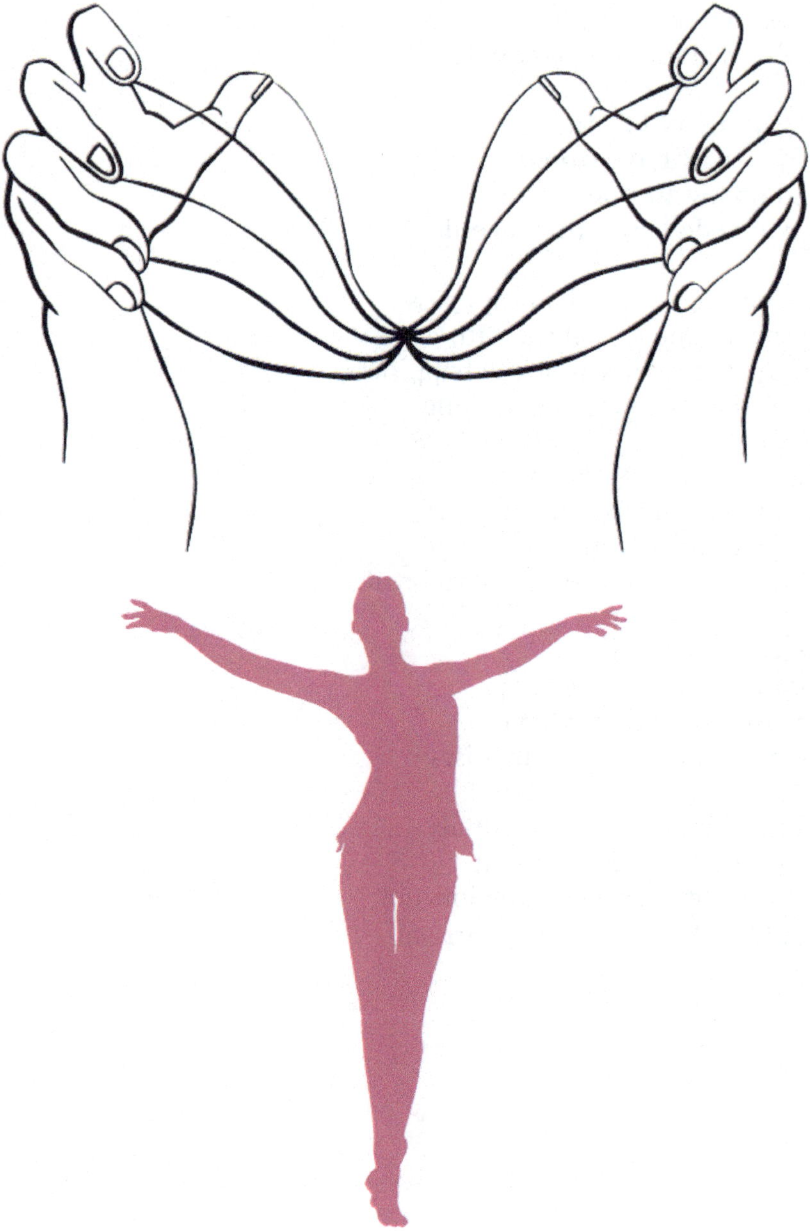

No Hands

Look Mom! No Hands!
Because I can stand alone on my own.

And Look Mom! No Man!
Because I expand from what I've outgrown.
No asshole zone.

Just look at all this land.
Because that man was just quicksand.
I was dangling by his strand.
His wish was my command.
So, my flesh bore his brand.

God laughs when we make plans.

So, I embrace the unknown.
Like a Queen on my throne.
Heart muscles nice & toned.

Sticks & stones may break my bones
But, from his rejection I have grown.
You can't un-sew what's been sewn
So, I'll stand alone on my own.

Foundation of cement, not sand
So, Look Mom, No hands

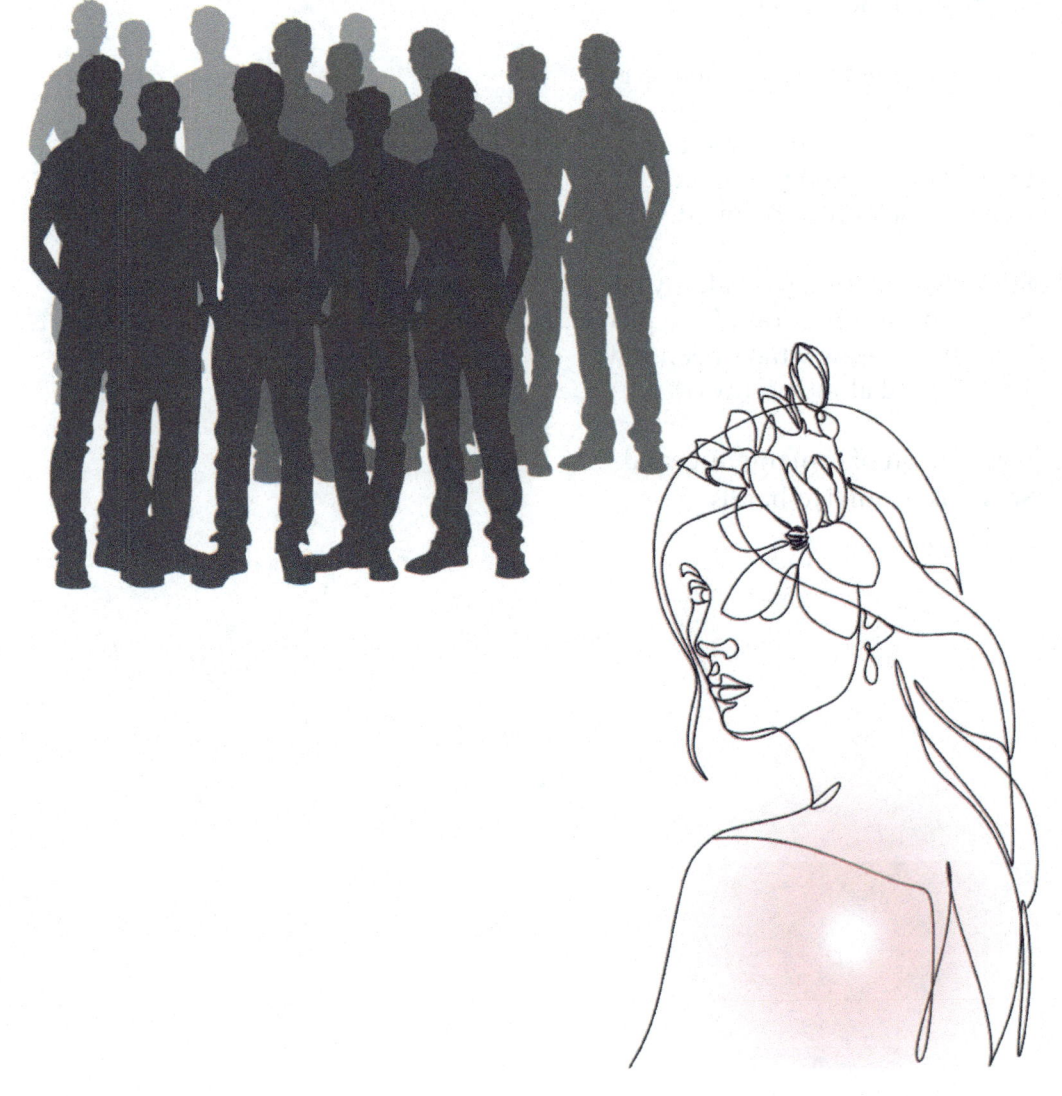

The Remedy

Born with a disease and searching my whole life for the cure
You came along and opened my heart wider than ever before
But people are fallible, if anything at all, that I know for sure
Connection is beautiful, but with attachment, I am always wanting more

Months of self-constructed torment brought me to my knees weeping
The pain of losing our connection was unbearable- cue the endless sleeping
But, the warrior inside me would not fold -nagging like a constant beeping
She had a vital message, the cure for my disease she had been keeping

She said, "The antidote you seek to heal what is within,"
"You will never find it, in the words or arms of men"
"For years you have made some man a being of supremacy"
"But, sweet girl, you have overlooked your power - You are The Remedy."

My eyes became wells for all my tears and their wishes
Got my needle and thread to sew my heart some self-love stitches
The little girl inside me that I have abandoned and betrayed for years
Crawled out from her dark corner, hand in hand we could face our fears

Now, when we are afraid we look inside or above
There is a never-ending peace found in both self and God's love
I wouldn't trade my best days with you for this healing and serenity
Because you were always the placebo, and I was looking for The Remedy

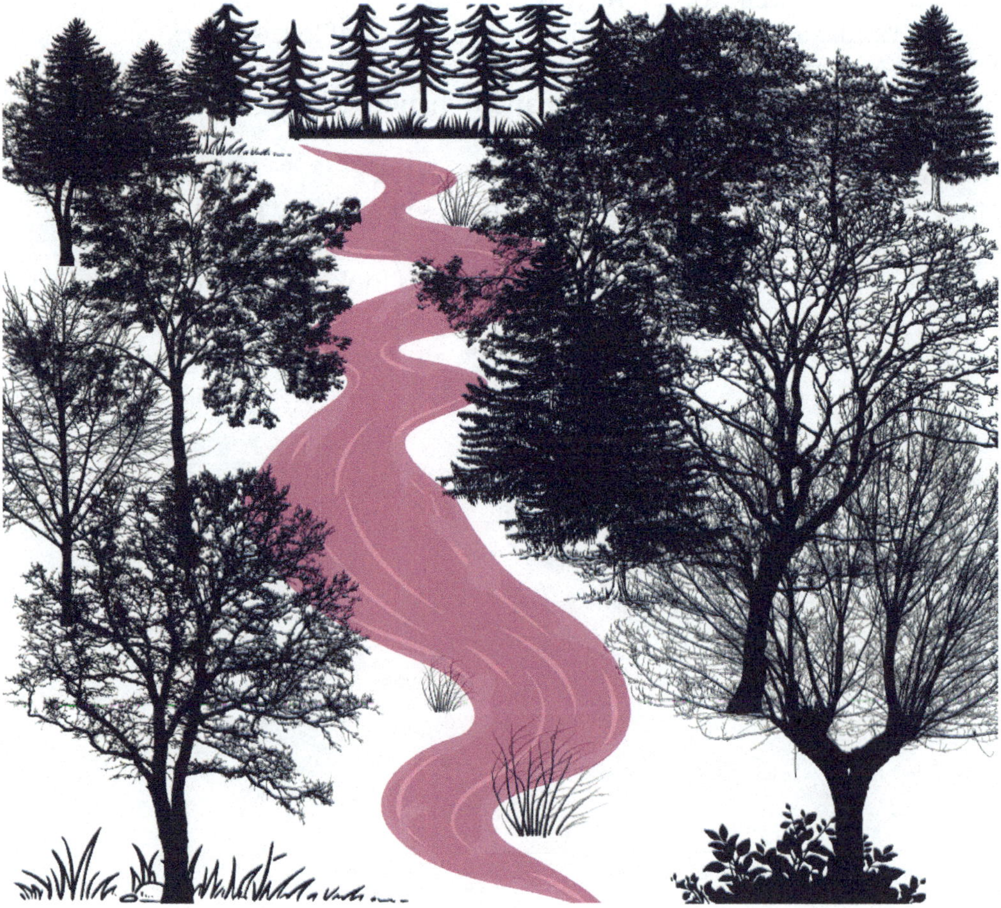

River

I found myself lost in the woods
In Her heart flowed a River, misunderstood

Many times, in those woods, I walked within
Yet, that miraculous River never had been

The chill of His water, down my spine, sent a shiver
"He is afraid of your warmth," the Jasmine whispered

Pulled to his current, praying "thy will be done"
Unafraid of his frost, for He can reflect the Sun

Floating, drifting, at peace in His mystical waters
Staring up in wonder, imagining His alluring Autumns

The colors change & the emotions are fleeting
When He avoids the rain, His banks start retreating

I struggle & fight, drowning myself to swim upstream
But, His rapids taught me that forced peace is not redeemed

Ashamed, defeated, worried He would send me downriver
But, He was raised by The Tree of Life, the infinite giver

Seasons pass, and His water flows stronger
In His own time, His fear he was able to conquer

I lost myself, found in the woods
In Her heart flowed a River, only I understood

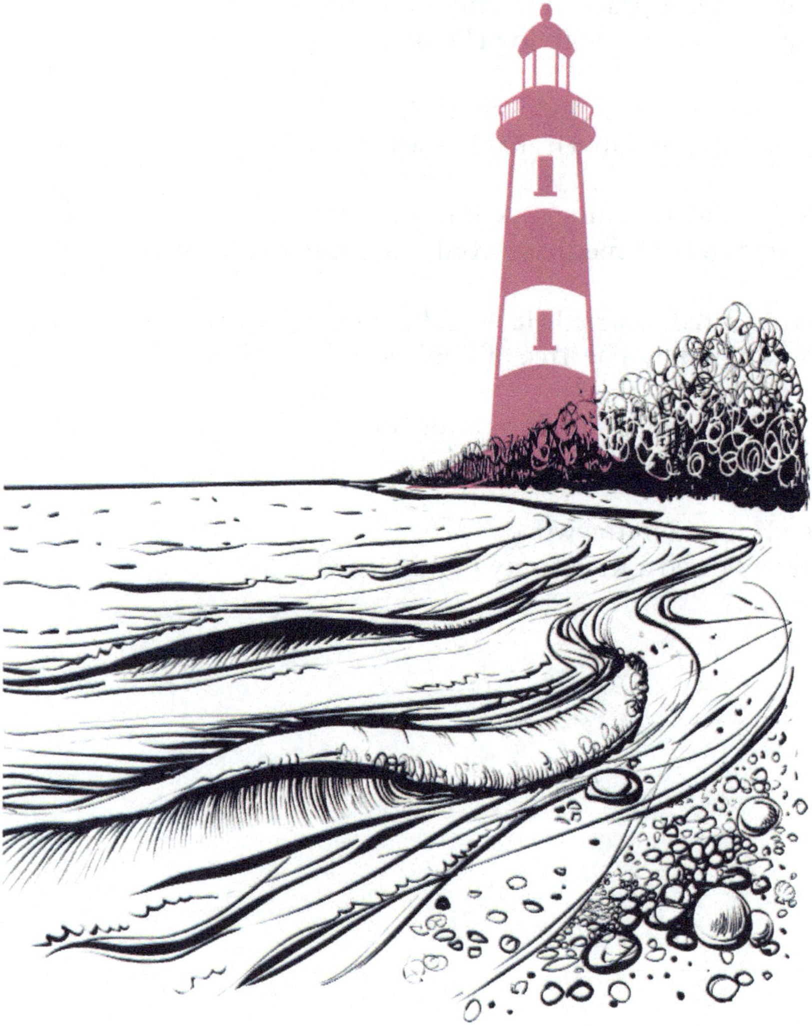

Giver. Of. Direction.

A push, a pull, a tug
I am here
A subtle warmth lost in the breeze
Tense and release

In the Hollow Ache
Heart leaks spout
To make room for His peace
Tense and release

Usher of pain
Conductor of power
Healer of disease
Tense and release

Guide. Of. Decisions.
Grower. Of. Devotion.
Giver. Of. Dreams.
Tense and release

Lighthouse of the soul
I am here
Worshipping your Sandy shore
To my prison I held the key
Tense and release

A push, a pull, a tug
I live here
Knowing and direction
Like ripened fruit on the trees

Fallen to my knees
I am released
I am liberated
I am free

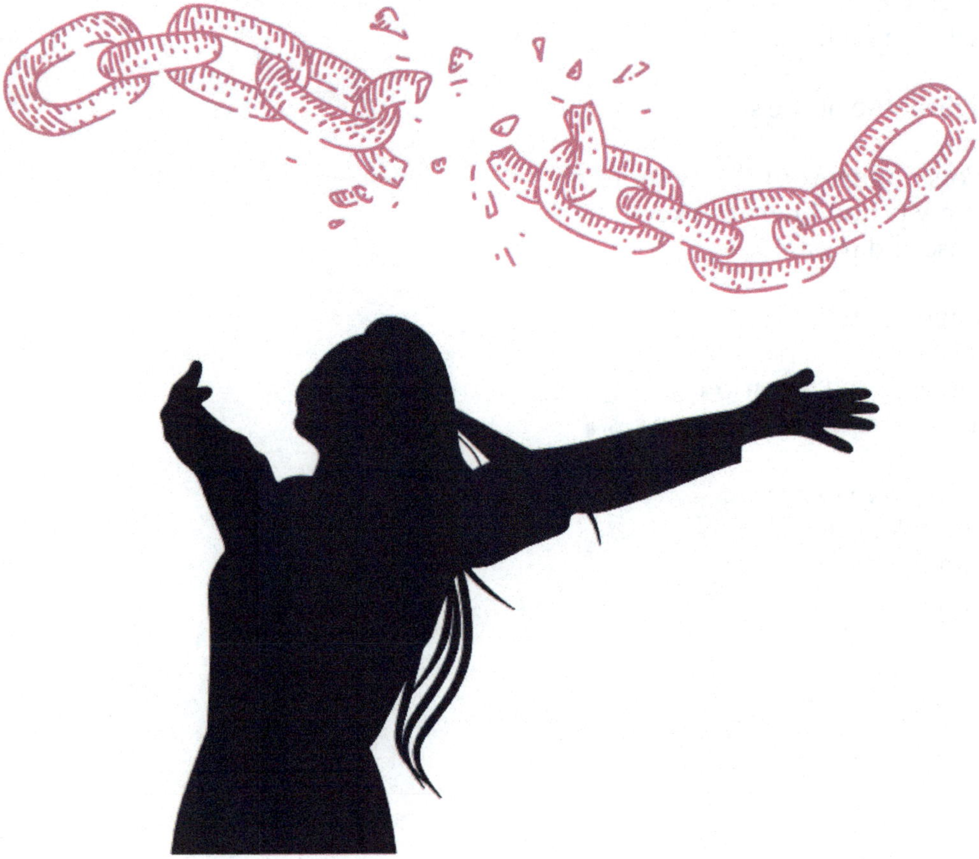

Liberation

Broken & defeated, I needed a transformation
Not for a lack of trying, I had motivation
Taking suggestions to fuel my determination
With death all around me, it was time for creation

Fell to my knees and made a decision
God then appeared in the form of a vision
All this time, I was fighting the opposition
But, I held the key to my self-made prison

It was about time for me to change my station
The tools in my belt, can't buy that education
God as my Employer, I had a new occupation
He forgave my sins, not worried about reputation

Love in my heart, I'm on a new mission
True service to others not for recognition
Channeling His peace like a kind of intuition
Freedom fits me nicely, I like this edition

This isn't the end, just building a foundation
Can't get complacent, it's a rededication
I finally understand the meaning of salvation
It's next level - a complete spiritual elevation

God as my Broker I get serenity as commission
Everyday isn't perfect, I'll make the admission
Strengthening a muscle, all about repetition
It's yours if you want it, don't need my permission

Everyday I'm grateful I had this revelation
Blessed to be God's living demonstration
I'll let you have your own interpretation
There's no "one size fits all" when it comes to liberation

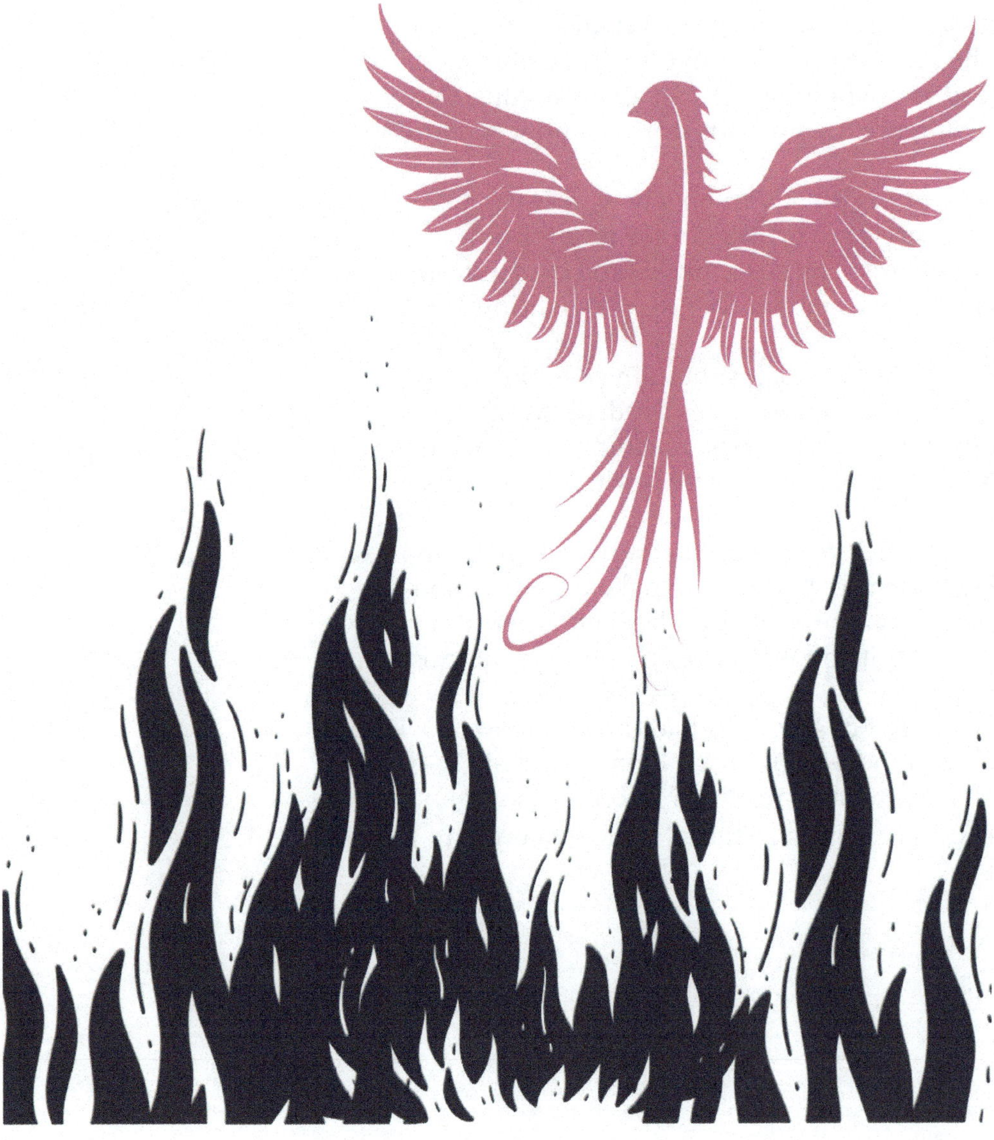

Rebirth

Eyes closed, heart opened
Deep sleep, subconscious mind
Tree of life, vibrant colors
In my pain, God gave a sign

A revival is to improve & strengthen
The person I have always been
Seeing the destruction in my rearview
I know I must be born again

Like the phoenix from the ashes
I will rebuild and mold myself
God's love and a higher calling
Never betraying for someone else

Resilience has new meaning
Withstanding more than I thought I could
In the suffering, came His peace
A pain that hurt so good

And from the womb of heartbreak
I am delivered into healing
With an unwavering sense of self
Other identities I am done stealing

The fulfillment I thought I needed
Was just the Devil's old folktale
My love is what I craved the most
Other attempts were an epic fail

I will not relinquish my magic
For now, I know my worth
Rest in Pieces, to that lifeless girl
Let us Thank God for my rebirth

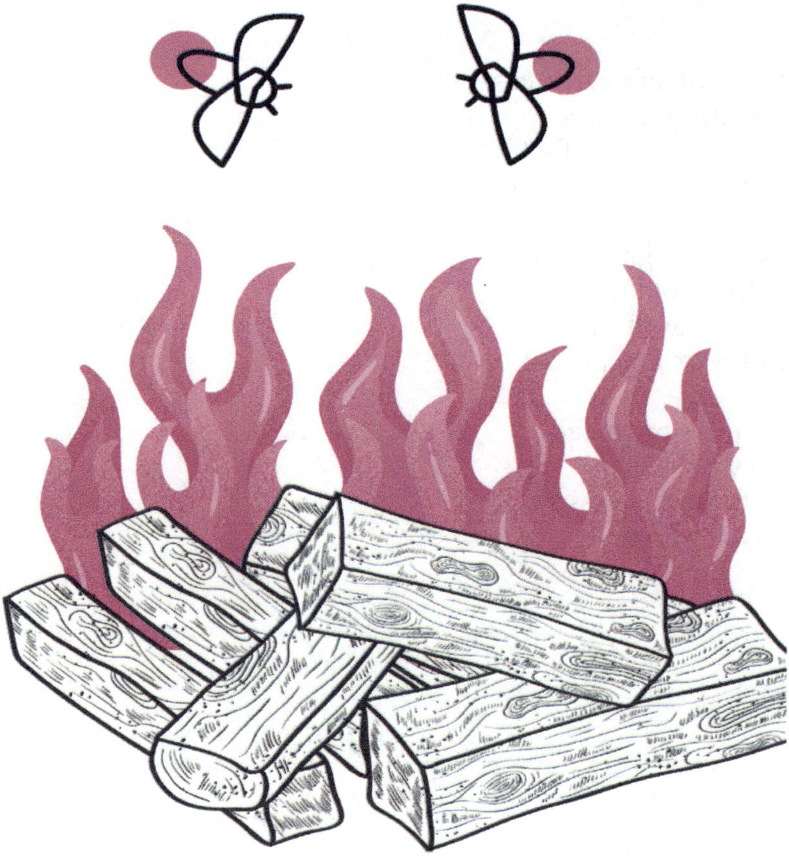

Sister

You're the one that understands me
Like the ocean and the sand
Laughing at stories of the seagulls
Connecting over dreams of dry land

In many ways we are different
And in much more we are the same
Just like the lightning bugs and fireflies
We are the same soul with two names

In the moments I have lost myself
You're the light that guides me home
If you had never looked for me
Alone on the streets I would roam

When the world and her people
Get terribly cold and jaded
You build the fire that keeps us warm
The frost is always barricaded

My life has had some heartache
My drive through pain, I took the scenic
They say blood is thicker than water
Well, jokes on them because I'm anemic

This is not about the sister I lost
Although, I have greatly missed her
No, this one here is all about
The friends that became my sisters

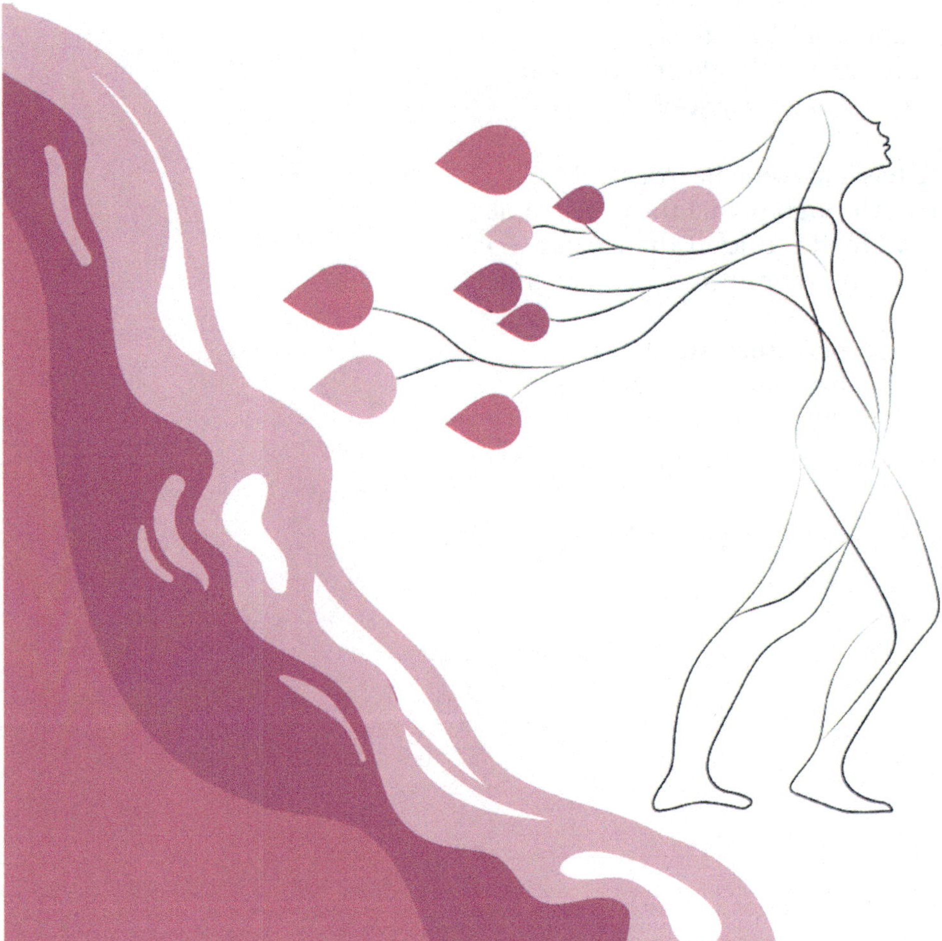

Water

I always thought being a liquid made me weak
A fluid among the solid, made me despise my leaks

Others were forceful and strong in their convictions
But their walls were disguised fear that caused them many restrictions

I used to wish I was a gas and could disappear into the air
That I could have an escape, a moment of relief from despair

Those vapors, however, cannot be seen or felt
They just float through life, sometimes only being smelled

I am flowing, fluid, rushing and gushing
A deep, blue ocean and a forest creek's hushing

I can stand on my own like the lakes and rivers
I can contribute to life as one of Mother Nature's givers

I am strong enough to put out a wild fire
For a penny and a wish, I can grant your deepest desire

My form allows me to be flexible with life's infinite surprises
I just curve the river bank when anything unsavory arises

I am gentle, smooth, and soft on your skin
But, I am capable of flooding if I need to wash away your sins

I am many extremes that I cannot conceal
Without this duality, I would not be real

I am not the perfect daughter
And, for my parents, I am stronger
I never wanted to be an author
And, God had me think broader
I resent my sister because I lost her
And, she'd be sick even if I sought her
My inner child thought I crossed her
And I'm sorry for the suffering I caused her

This is the new me, molded in pain, at God's altar
Nothing about it was easy, every step of the way, I fought her
I am grateful for the lesson each agonizing heartbreak taught her
I just wanted to be seen, but even I never saw her
The fire didn't harden me, it just made my heart softer

My power is, I am love, abundant love, with infinite love to offer
I give away, but I'm never depleted- like an endless life force, I am water

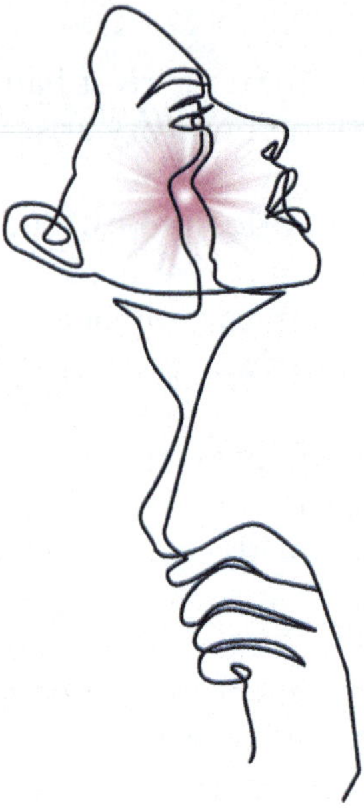
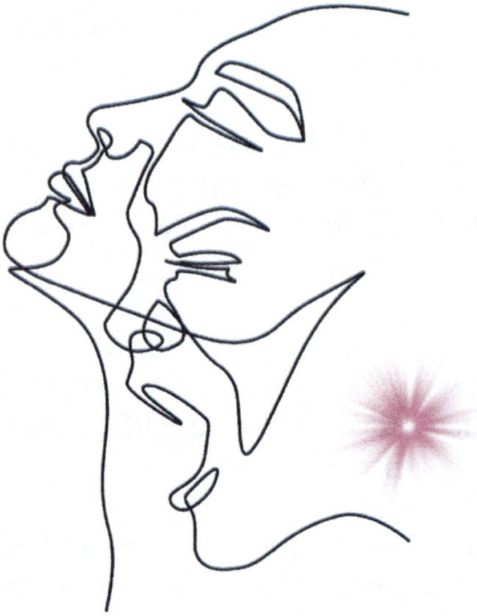
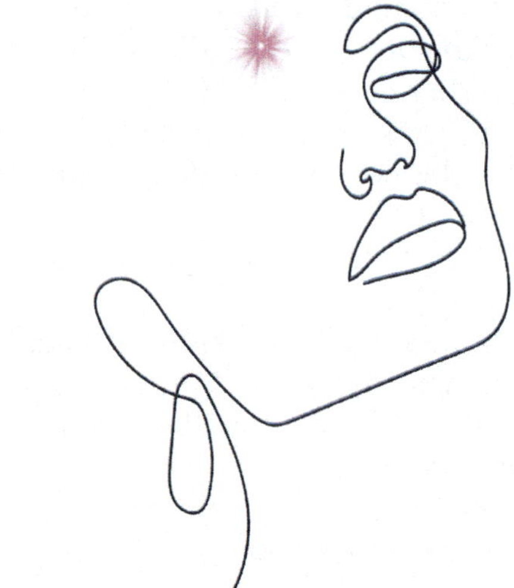
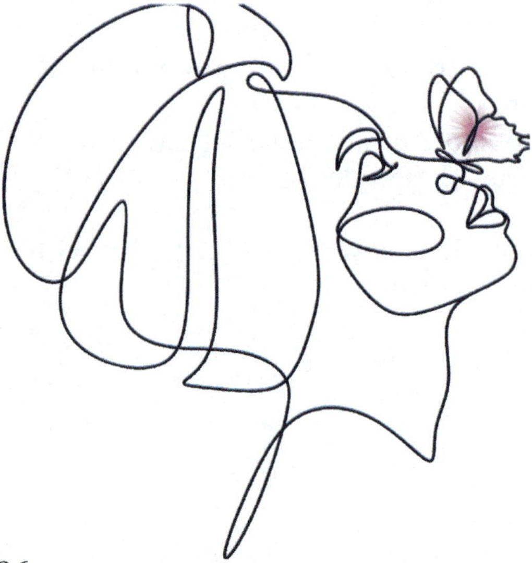

Answer Key

1. Grief: Who is She? .... HONESTY
2. Anger: Who is She? .... FEAR
3. Initiation: Who is He? .... HUMILITY
4. Nirvana: Who is He? .... FAITH

Made in the USA
Coppell, TX
23 March 2025